Brand
Together

Brand Together

How co-creation generates innovation and re-energizes brands

Nicholas Ind
Clare Fuller
Charles Trevail

KoganPage

LONDON PHILADELPHIA NEW DELHI

First published in Great Britain and the United States in 2012 by Kogan Page Limited

120 Pentonville Road	1518 Walnut Street, Suite 1100	4737/23 Ansari Road
London N1 9JN	Philadelphia PA 19102	Daryaganj
United Kingdom	USA	New Delhi 110002
www.koganpage.com		India

© Nicholas Ind, Clare Fuller and Charles Trevail, 2012

ISBN   978 0 7494 6325 0
E-ISBN 978 0 7494 6326 7

British Library Cataloguing-in-Publication Data

A CIP record for this book is available from the British Library.

Library of Congress Cataloging-in-Publication Data

Ind, Nicholas.
   Brand together : how co-creation generates innovation and re-energizes brands / Nicholas Ind, Clare Fuller, Charles Trevail. – 1st ed.
      p. cm.
   Includes bibliographical references and index.
   ISBN 978-0-7494-6325-0 – ISBN 978-0-7494-6326-7
1. Product management. 2. Branding (Marketing) 3. Customer relations. I. Fuller, Clare.
II. Trevail, Charles. III. Title.
   HD69.B7I526 2012
   658.4'063–dc23
                              2011040582

Typeset by Macmillan Publishing Solutions
Printed and bound in India by Replika Press Pvt Ltd

CONTENTS

ACKNOWLEDGEMENTS

This book has been written with the help of:

Dr Nick Coates

Felix Koch

Doron Meyassed

and with participation from:

Alain Samson – Independent Researcher

Andy Stubbings – The Futures Company

Asa Dotzler – Mozilla

Ben Hayman – Promise

Benedikt Langner – Saïd Business School

Bill Walshe – The Doyle Collection

Brian Millar – Sense Worldwide

Cecile Lux – Danone

Cristian Saracco – Allegro234

Christof Zürn – Creative Companion

Claire Claxton – Etihad

Erik Zsiga – Electrolux

George Penman – Barclays Bank

Dr Graham Hill – Independent Consultant

Guy Crawford – Jumeirah

Henrik Otto – Electrolux

Henrik Sjödin – Stockholm School of Economics

Ian Hallsworth – Kogan Page

Jaco van Zijll Langhout – Capgemini Consulting

Jan Bosch – Intuit

Jennifer Kitchen – Promise

John Elkins – First Data

Jon Finch – Kogan Page

Libby Nutt – Casella Wines

Lilli Allihn – Promise

Louise Burke – more! Magazine

Louise Dolding – Promise

Lucy Green – Greenfields Communications

Maarten Korz – Rabobank

Marcia Mihotich – Mihotich Design

Mark Putt – Tata Global Beverages

Martin Scott – KPMG

Nick Bonney – Everything Everywhere

Nina Croad – Greenfields Communications

Oriol Iglesias – ESADE, Barcelona

Patrick Harris – The Futures Company

Peggy Curley – ING

Perry Yeatman – Kraft Foods

Phil Raby-Smith – Independent Consultant

Rick Jenner – Virgin Media

Ruth Mortimer – Marketing Week

Dr Sheila Keegan – Campbell Keegan

Stephan Durach – BMW

Teresa Lynch – MrWeb

YF Juan - ITRI

Brand Together Community

amandawright(e)	Earlobes	hudswell	polarpat22
FriendlyLynn	meee	bucksfizz66	tjpoppleton
yvonne14	JohnHoward-Norfolk	pontelad	pedrapislwyn
tozza27		Dizzy	IceBerG
clararhea	bradbury	paulpry118	Helenbackagain
davidclee	tigs	elliemac	smileypantsjo
chukki	jane	littlestaramy	nicky22
madge	michaeladkins	pegleg	Irwin

tea
Doreen3127
bunny
jongorton
DaveJames
abdelmoutaleb
pieeater
Fenny
jps
cornflower
WHAMMO
Katie
jennyreeve
fatoldtart
tigerdigs
xnatx
sas77
effiem
catkeys
lesleyc
Triciajoy
vickynn
tigerbabe68
xavier
NoCowOn-TheHorizon
fatha
pmf1966
Stretchnecks
TinaM
clarabel1968
boszorder
gaylardsl
aladin
daddyede
hoppyloo
savvysaver
bankse
narrowboat owner

kjlb
lisa4462
auditbabe
princesskitten
murraysmith1975
deco105
pinkbooty121
philster
hello999
apitman
rhi1972
radun10
Big M
Villordsutch
Ranger
kitkat
saffron25
Pip
Speaks99
tddarkangel
tiffenymonson
vicki83
Qexit
nuska
Dan Lambskin
dorsetman
BOBBYNIC
MissDaisy
danny
dainorka
puru83
maggiemay
Aster
dxi256
adrianrelward
MTDancer
wendybalzan
alison
wendabell

Kitt120
rw87
thankfulsal
Pembroke
alangb
hazey3
lomasw2
BlackWoodpecker
Guccigirl
chackwith
vrwatters
jewren
sam135
SarahPascall
East End Girl
Geniusima
f1re_cr4cker
ianrick
Mazza
aguarino
jkerry
Junebug
purplecoconut17
MrBloggs
shopping.uk
trayrope
denisehayes
suze26
dvavasour
jaz1919
ladyp
chrish
WWright20
radley
yaffle
missy
pyknic
Northatlantic99
charliegreat

annabrett
Beautifaal
FabulousCity
Mary
Donadee416
hollychops
dollyd010
Lolo
Magrit
jillmcintyre
jennifer122105
jtrought
geoff4985
Dc22112
jetset717
audann
BWin11
mansemob
pat mitchell
piemanji
isisleeds
redjune
chris55
Alan Hawkes
LEDave
PopCart
jennyg
bje
dragonfly63
joolzcook
billsteamshovel
fastein
lissy
staceyk84
1289
magoogy
rkieda
tuggsy
cliveoverlander

sirjohn	nancy	covlad76	debz1989
incasneighbour	rogerb	sherv1978	anniemagic1
Alex	linda	NickFollows	TheComing-
scottc1978	dkmalster	Molly	Gnomes
bluestarrz	mark	charbarritt	leanne1987
eastend	lclollipop	gbrittsf	saffron56
ohmissjones	esmereynolds	gail	Elbandito
mikeengineer	hanatan	Georgiajls	dsavery
greyfox1	hijigu	iallan	vavrath
spd	Helenb5241	inkrey	deano
maggy4	nicola953	daz963	

The Brand Together community was managed and facilitated by Joe Stubbs and Sean Bone at Promise

Introduction

Most leaders would like their organizations to be more innovative: to create new products and services; to develop inventive business processes; to change the rules and boundaries of a market; indeed to follow in the footsteps of pioneers such as Apple, Google and Virgin. Their motivation, apart from a desire to emulate these business successes, is that consumers and other stakeholders demand the relevantly new. Correctly understanding and meeting people's needs and wants drives successful innovation: think Apple iPad, Google Earth and Virgin Media's Digital Home Support. For these businesses, innovation is a top strategic priority that delivers value for customers and generates above average returns. As James Andrew of Boston Consulting Group notes of the 50 most innovative companies in the world, 'they outperform their regional peers in stock markets somewhere north of 200 basis points, year after year.' So we might ask, why don't more organizations invest in innovation? Yet throwing money at it doesn't seem to be the answer. There is no statistically significant relationship between the spend on innovation and financial performance. Steve Jobs also made the point in an interview with Fortune (1998) when he said, 'innovation has nothing to do with how many R&D dollars you have.'

Success in innovation is really rooted in two key areas. First is the insight into people's whole lives – not just their consuming lives. This means digging deep below the way people explain the surface of things through language to the more difficult to express limbic emotions, feelings and memory that determine behaviour. For example, if we take that oft quoted phrase of Henry Ford's, 'if I had asked people what they wanted, they would have said a faster horse', we can make the point, as Ford is doing, that you don't get innovation as a result of talking to people. Yet, what he really illustrates is that if you ask such a question you will get a rational answer. To get deeper you have to ask why and then people might respond with thoughts about convenience, connecting with others, staying in touch with friends and making best use of one's time. Go deeper again and you might get some further associations and memories of speed and childhood and community – a Proustian meandering into the past and a sense of what people would like in the future. The importance of customer insight is illustrated by the research into successful innovators. In an annual study of 1,000 companies, Barry Jaruzelski and Kevin Dehoff write that the best organizations depend on a common set of critical innovation capabilities: the ability to gain insights into customer needs, an understanding of the potential relevance of emerging technologies at the ideation phase, active engagement with customers to prove the validity of concepts during product development and working with pilot users to roll out products carefully during commercialization.

The challenge here for organizations has been in achieving the insight that drives innovation. Cocooned inside the walls of the business and limited by cultural blinkers, managers can easily lose the ability to understand customer motivations. This lack of connection is usually compensated for by market research, but quantitative and qualitative research is often ignored or misused. It also has some limitations in getting to the emotions, feelings and future intentions that drive innovation, because research is an approximation of a current situation based on the past and creates abstract information which is mistaken for the real.[1] In *Brand Together* we advocate that organizations should try to get closer to customers and other stakeholders; to reduce the distance by encouraging participation and co-creation. In this line of thought we go beyond the traditional idea of asking people to argue rationally what they might do and instead ask them to just do it. This is about events and communities where people can explore together questions and answers and where managers can take part in a dialogue of ideation and development; where, as Mark Watts-Jones of Orange suggests, you can be surprised by the difference between how as managers you imagine people live, use services and connect with their friends, and the reality.

The second element that is vital to innovation is the capacity of the organization to focus on what it is good at and to make those difficult choices about what and what not to do. 'Most successful companies, we found, are those that focus on a particular, narrow set of common and distinctive capabilities that enable them to better execute their chosen strategy.'[2] The implication here is that the organization needs to look inwards and to understand itself, which brings us to a word that is rarely used in the books and articles on innovation: branding. It is as though the word is taboo for innovators. Maybe it is because brands and branding are still dominantly associated with logos, packaging and advertising and brands are often seen as ephemeral and possibly manipulative. In the innovation arena the people who matter are social anthropologists, engineers, product designers and scientists – not branders. Yet if we understand 'brand' as a set of ideas that define why an organization (or product or service) exists, how it does things and what it produces, we might be able to overcome the myopia around brands and realize the brand creates a focus and framework for innovation. For example, the core brand idea of Virgin as the 'people's champion', and a set of values that includes the word 'fun' defines a certain lens for viewing innovation that would preclude an innovation that aligned with the status quo and was unfun. New products and services from Virgin are meant to challenge the way things are.

So, this book is a journey into the world of innovation from the perspective of the brand. In other words, we will explore how a brand idea (the implicit or explicit definition of the brand) creates a certain set of possibilities to be realized by a certain set of actions that are distinctive to the organization. Equally this book is a journey into the human mind and body and is based on the belief that innovation must be human-centric – enabling the realization of people's dreams and aspirations by involving them in the creation and development of the very things that affect their lives. This is not to deny the power of the creative genius who invents a new technology or product, but more to argue that we cannot always rely on the intuition of the inventor, who may be good at producing something technically more efficient but not always so good at creating something people want to buy. For that we need to use the intelligence and creativity of the individuals who buy and use brands, for it is when we bring diverse minds together that we discover the new. As Steve Johnson argues about large groups in *Where Good Ideas Come From*, it is not the crowd itself that becomes wise, but rather that connected individuals become smarter.[3]

During this odyssey, we will look at what co-creation is, where it has come from and why it is becoming a more widely used means of idea generation and implementation – something noted in IBM's 2010 study of more than 1,500 CEOs, where it is observed that 'the most successful organizations co-create products and services with customers, and integrate customers into core processes'.[4] We will also discuss how to use the framework of the brand and the tools of co-creation in practice and the structural and cultural implications. We will look at the limits of participative innovation and the difficulties of involving large numbers of people in a brand dialogue and the benefits of co-creation in terms of the quality of ideas and the speed of adoption and traction they gain inside organizations. Throughout the book we will illustrate our ideas with case studies and examples and feature some of the practical steps you can take to experiment successfully with your brand.

Notes

1 Ronell, A (2005) *The Test Drive*. University of Illinois Press, Urbana and Chicago

2 Jaruzelski, B and Dehoff, K (2010) 'The Global Innovation 1000: How the Top Innovators Keep Winning.' *Strategy+Business* **61**

3 Johnson, S (2010) *Where Good Ideas Come From: The Natural History of Innovation*, Allen Lane, London.

4 IBM: Capitalizing on Complexity. Research based on 1,541 face-to-face interviews with CEOs worldwide between September 2009 and January 2010.

PART ONE
Thinking it

Brand Together is split into two parts: a philosophical part comprising the first three chapters and then a practical 'doing it' part comprising the rest of the book. Structurally this seems to make sense because the idea of co-creation and its relationship to branding needs to have some sort of definition and also context, before we discuss the application. However, it is clear that the two sections have strong areas of overlap and the distinction between them in practice is nebulous as the principles and action scud back and forward. Does thinking determine the action or does the action define the thinking? Whichever way we understand this process, the important thing to recognize is that we are part of our worlds, so nothing ever takes place in a vacuum. To help reflect this, the first section covers not only the concept of co-creation but also features examples of organizations and their practices. The content for this (as throughout the book) has been derived from several sources. First, we have drawn on a wide range of published material. This is diverse because we believe co-creation, in thought and in practice, draws on different disciplines. In addition to branding literature we refer to sources from philosophy, psychology, anthropology, creativity, art, literature and innovation. Second, we have conducted in-depth interviews with 20 managers from around the world who have taken part in co-creation processes. Their ideas and experiences permeate the book. Third, in June 2011, we organized a working session around the draft of the book with a group of co-creation experts who provided invaluable input on the material. Fourth, there are inserts within the book from other writers who offer specific slants on relevant topics. Finally, some 236 individuals agreed to participate in a moderated community tasked with helping to co-create the future of co-creation.

In Part One, we will look at three themes. In Chapter 1 we address the problem of the vagueness and misuse of the idea of co-creation and specify the key ingredients as we see them. Inevitably this requires us to say what co-creation is not and to challenge the way it is conflated with co-production, open innovation, crowdsourcing and other terms that float around. We put forward the view that co-creation must embrace four connected ideas: participation, openness, empowerment and organizational involvement. In being specific we largely exclude areas that are important, such as naturally-occurring communities and user-generated content, because they do not involve the organization and the individual working directly together. In Chapter 2 we show that innovation must be connected to the brand. This is inevitable, even if not always realized. The brand which frames the co-creation process always inspires and limits managers and customers, while the outputs of the process also impact on the brand as it is stretched in new directions through new products and services. Chapter 3 then covers the different approaches to co-creation, from those organizations that have embraced it as a way of life, to the experimenters and on to the rejectors. In the last category, we include organizations that simply lack the will or the capability to get closer to customers and also those that have rejected co-creation because they have found approaches they believe are better for connecting with customers in a productive way. We are enthusiasts for co-creation, but it may not be appropriate for all contexts and we should recognize therefore the value of different perspectives.

The final point to note about the book is that it tries throughout to balance the perspectives of the individual and the organization. When writing a book that is designed for a business readership there is always a tendency to see issues and problems from the perspective of the organization. Yet, especially in a book on co-creation, that needs to be balanced. If co-creation is genuinely about getting close to customers and other stakeholders, then we need to see things from their perspective as well. This a constant feature of the book and part of the reason why it has itself been co-created by community members and experts.

Creating the future together

Innovation has always been a group activity. The myth of the lone genius having a eureka moment that changes the world is indeed a myth. Most innovation is the result of long hours building on the input of others . . . If you're comfortable with the language of memes, you could say a healthy meme needs an ecosystem not of a single brain, but of a network of brains. That's how ideas bump into other ideas, replicate, mutate, and evolve.[1]

Before we can look at the way co-creation works to deliver brand-led innovation, we need to understand what it is. The word itself does of course give us a sense of its meaning: the idea of creativity developed together with others. This is distinct from another commonly used phrase, co-production. Co-creation suggests the interaction of individuals within a framework to evolve, re-define or invent something that is new. In contrast, co-production suggests the involvement of people in the process of production.

To illustrate the difference, we can look at NikeiD, a platform that enables customers to tailor-make their running shoes. At NikeiD, you can alter sizes, choose colours and inscribe your name. It provides an interesting opportunity to personalize a mass market brand that has long stressed the idea of personal empowerment, but it is no different in substance from a bespoke service that creates made-to-measure clothing. It is not co-creation but a return to the world before mass consumer goods came to dominate, where products were made to order. What would constitute co-creation in this context is customers taking part in face-to-face and/or online sessions to discuss their needs and, in partnership with Nike, designing, prototyping and producing a new running shoe that is sold to other consumers. The interesting point here is that this is exactly where Nike started. When the company that would become Nike was established by the University of Oregon track coach, Bill Bowerman and one of his runners, Phil Knight, in 1964, the focus was on selling running shoes to athletes. To develop relevant products that enhanced performance, Jeff Johnson, the company's first employee, would go to track events, talk to the runners about their needs, get their ideas and then organize prototypes. Bill Bowerman would also be at the trackside adjusting the shoes and shaving off any excess leather to reduce weight. This is how Nelson Farris (employee number 18) describes it: 'We were all terrified we were going to go broke, because we were such a small company. But we innovated and experimented. We'd listen to runners, go and try things out and sometimes come back within 24 hours and let the runner use it. So through that listening, that instantaneous feedback, through taking risks and trying to invent product we were able to do things way different from anybody else.'

So, in the early days, Nike's customers were active participants in a journey of discovery; the co-creators of the Nike brand. At the professional sports level that process still continues. Speed skating suits, soccer boots and golfing equipment, for example, utilize the knowledge and creativity of athletes and sportsmen and women and are developed in participation with them. From Nike's perspective this provides a connectivity and deep insight into the emotional needs of the individual and the practical requirements of performance. The dialogue that co-creation facilitates enables the company to develop prototypes that can be road-tested by the athlete, generating further feedback and the potential for refinement. It is this iterative process that is one of the distinguishing features of co-creation.

If an organization really wants to generate insight into customers' lives and engage with their passions and ideas it involves more than just tiptoeing round colour and style choices, even though they might be appealing in themselves. A business that wants to experiment with or even embrace co-creation needs to enter into a partnership with its customers and other stakeholders and allow them real influence. The implication of this is that to generate the value that co-creation can provide, an organization needs to understand four key aspects of the process that sit underneath the umbrella of the brand. We will now look at each of these in turn.

Co-creation is participative

There are two prevalent myths about creativity and innovation. The first is that creativity is the preserve of the individual creative genius. The second is that innovations are generated by eureka moments, often from people in scientific or computer laboratories. These myths exist because they are more interesting to narrate, not least by those credited with discoveries, but if we look beneath the surface we often find that innovations are developed by groups of people and that they usually take a long time to become fully formed, which reminds us that innovations are not just about the big idea but all the small ideas of innovation development. Steve Johnson, in an analysis of innovations since 1400, concludes that 'less than 10 percent of innovation during the Renaissance is networked; two centuries later a majority of breakthrough ideas emerge in collaborative environments.'[2] In other words, while we may have a picture in our heads of innovation as a solitary activity, it is in fact a social one. Johnson references a study by the researcher Kevin Dunbar who was interested in the nature of scientific discoveries and videotaped the activities of scientists in their laboratories. He found that most of their discoveries were not made sitting looking through a micrcoscope or poring over data, but rather in informal meetings and discussions with colleagues. Similarly, take the film production company, Pixar, which has produced a string of hit films, such as Toy Story, Cars, The Incredibles and WALL-E. The company, in recognizing the need for continuous creativity, deliberately creates opportunities for people to sit together and discuss ideas. There are periodic reviews and post-mortems, but most important are the 'dailies' – an open feedback session where work is shown and discussed. This helps to ensure the involvement of diverse perspectives and to maintain high levels of detailed creativity: 'the director and the other creative leaders of a production do not come up with all the ideas on their own; rather every single member of the 200–250 person production group makes suggestions. Creativity must be present at every level of every artistic and technical part of the organization.'[3]

These examples are illustrations of Kleist's phrase, '*L'idée vient en parlant.*' It was Kleist's point in his 1805 essay 'On the Gradual Production of Thoughts While Speaking'[4] that we can sit alone in our room trying to solve a seemingly intractable problem and then when we talk to others, suddenly the answer is there. As Johnson says, 'an idea is a network.' It is formed out of associations with other ideas and developed with and for others. This suggests that we are unlikely to maximize the innovation potential of an organization if the generation of new ideas is the preserve of an elite or if we rely on abstract data to connect us with customers. Rather we should be working to involve as many people as possible in the organization in idea generation and development – to recognize the distinction that Amabile and Khaire (2008) make, that leaders should not manage creativity but manage *for* creativity.[5] And we should also be working to engage with external stakeholders such that they also become part of the process of creation. Businesses ought to be encouraging their people to get out more, both in a literal sense in creating the opportunity for employees to meet and talk with customers, but also using online mechanisms to create communities of exchange.

This principle of participation is hardly a new idea. In the 18th century, coffee houses were places that enabled ideas to network. For example, in London people came together, drank coffee, invented new ideas and co-created the Enlightenment. By 1739, there were 551 coffee houses (the total population was around 700,000) and they were central in creating networks of connected individuals.[6] Interestingly, coffee houses have again become a place of participation. Visit a coffee house in Pala Alto or Mountain View in Silicon Valley and you will see people replicating the activities of their 18th-century predecessors as they share ideas, pitch business concepts and create partnerships.

Online participation at Starbucks

Starbucks has become an emblem of the principle of participation. Starbucks coffee shops encourage lounging and conversation, although maybe not with the same apparent intensity or connectivity of those of the Enlightenment era. Indeed it seems ironic that a brand built on the idea of a conversational environment doesn't rely on face-to-face interaction as the main spur to innovation, but has instead adopted an online alternative: **www.mystarbucksidea.com**. Established in 2008, this is a community, facilitated by Starbucks, that encourages people to suggest ideas to improve the brand experience. Once posted, other community members can comment on ideas and either give them a thumbs up or thumbs down. Ideas that progress are nurtured by online idea partners – Starbucks employees trained to host discussions and bring resources to bear that can help with implementation. Both the quantity of ideas (70,000 in the first year) and the quality are interesting because people not only bring their coffee-drinking persona to the community, but their whole selves and their experiences as teachers, doctors, designers and scientists. It is this diversity of background and the sense of connection that makes the community viable. Cynically we might say that healthier sandwiches and free coffee for Gold Card members is not quite of the same level as inventing calculus or Newton's laws of motion, but it has rejuvenated Starbucks and cemented a strong feeling of connectedness between the brand and its customers. We could also point out that one of the great scientists of the Enlightenment, Joseph Priestley, was famous in his own lifetime partly because he invented soda water.

Co-creation is about openness

Since the 1970s 'numerous research projects have shown that successful innovation in a wide range of industries requires the integration of different productive domains – research, production, marketing – and the involvement of customers.'[7] Yet while research shows the value of involvement, organizations often struggle to involve others because they are still reliant on a controlled approach to innovation. This line of thought stresses the idea that value creation is the responsibility of the organization. It is organizational members, most often an elite group at a high level in the structure, that generate ideas and evolve new products and services which are then presented to consumers. The argument for this approach is that the level of expertise required to design and engineer a new car, for example, is such that it cannot be passed over to consumers. Indeed the more technical a product is, the greater the difficulty in involving consumers in the development process. Yet it is not impossible to involve others. People who have professional careers in associated disciplines such as design, architecture, ship science, ergonomics, can bring specific knowledge to a problem; consumers can provide insights into the way a product or service connects to their lives, and employees from different domains can make previously unseen connections: 'new mental structures, new constellations, come into being when knowledge, experiences, ideas from widely differing and distinct domains, meet.'[8]

The main barrier to the practice of co-creation is not really to do with technology but rather a belief in the expertise of key creative people inside the organization. It is a cultural issue based on an inward-looking approach that stresses the otherness of others. Andrea Gabor (2009) makes the point that employee engagement suffers for this very reason. 'Many Western companies have never been comfortable soliciting the opinions of employees, especially rank-and-file workers, in any systematic way. And few companies have been willing to make the long-term commitment that quality management entails.'[9] We might add that companies also struggle to engage with customers because they believe in a one-way process. They might absorb market research findings but the results are used to innovate internally and send the resulting outputs to customers. By contrast, co-creative organizations are two-way. They open themselves up to people inside and outside the organization and they take part in a conversation to learn and to change in a continuous process of development. This is what Baker, Jensen and Kolb describe as conversational learning. 'Conversational learning is expanded by distinct, yet intertwined, linear and cyclical processes that ultimately come together as the flux of spiral movements, as new ideas are advanced discursively and questioned from differing perspectives through recursive reconsiderations.'[10]

The underlying requirement for opening up the organization to enable co-creativity is the humility to recognize that good ideas are best developed by and with others. The reality is that customers are already talking about, using and sometimes innovating with the company's products. This creativity, whether expressed by individuals alone or in groups, can remain beyond the interest or influence of the organization, or alternatively the organization can engage with it, and learn together with its stakeholders. To make this shift requires the ability to trust people outside the organization and a willingness to share knowledge. This can be uncomfortable because it requires individuals to discard their prejudices, to allow seeming certainties to be questioned and to accept different viewpoints. This needs a recognition that value and meaning is created jointly, something that has come to be recognized by several writers.[11] Consumers increasingly want to be involved in the brands they like and admire, and technology increasingly enables companies to be involved in the lives of consumers.

How Generation C is driving acceptance of co-creation

The rapid development of first the Internet and then social media has been a key driver in the adoption of co-creation. Even if the forebears of co-creation date back before online connectivity, it is the emergence of Internet based communities that has really accelerated the opportunity for more interaction between customers and the organization. This looks set to continue, not least because the connected generation – Generation C – will continue to exert an influential role. Friedrich, Peterson and Koster describe the rapidly growing Generation C (people born after 1990) as connected, communicating, content-centric, computerized, community-oriented and always clicking. This group will make up 40 per cent of the population in the US, Europe and the BRIC countries by 2020. 'This is the first generation that has never known any reality other than that defined and enabled by the Internet, mobile devices, and social networking. . . More than 95 per cent of them have computers, and more than half use instant messaging to communicate, have Facebook pages, and watch videos on YouTube. Their familiarity with technology, reliance on mobile communications and desire to remain in contact with large networks of family members, friends, business contacts, and people with common interests, will transform how we work and how we consume.'[12]

This is a group that is brand aware and willing to participate, but it is also networked – comfortable with soliciting and offering opinions and ideas to others. The attitudes of Generation C are a powerful driver of co-creation, but as a group they also set a particular test for organizations. For the conversations between consumers and organizations to be productive, both sides need to learn to listen to each other and to establish relationships based on transparency and trust. From the company's perspective these are principles that cannot merely be espoused, but must be genuinely lived through the organization's actions.

Openness, transparency and trust at Mozilla

An example of an organization that really lives up to such ideas as openness, transparency and trust is the software company Mozilla. Based in

Mountain View, California, Mozilla has a stated mission to promote openness, innovation and opportunity on the web. This is a non-profit organization that grew out of Netscape and is involved in building communities of people that both help create and use their products such as the web browser Firefox and e-mail client Thunderbird. Mozilla employs a core group of some 300 people that develops software, manages processes and markets the products, but since the beginning much of the development has been due to the enthusiasm and commitment of customers who have become volunteers. In the early days of Mozilla, when it was up against a very dominant competitor in the form of Microsoft, there weren't enough resources internally. Software developers identified with the Mozilla philosophy, who gave up their spare time to develop products they themselves would like to use. They also saw an opportunity to work with smart people and solve difficult problems. Mozilla could of course have closed their doors to these would-be helpers but it would have shown that the principle of openness was just a veneer. Instead they embraced the principles of co-creation. Asa Dotzler of Mozilla says, 'by 2004 the majority of the code had been written by Netscape employees, but there were many hundreds of volunteers who played a substantial role in writing code including important features. For instance the first implementation of tabbed browsing was a volunteer-written code. Our first implementation of pop-up blocking and session restore when you crash, and lots of other key features, were developed by volunteers.' As well as these examples, Mozilla encouraged outsiders to help evolve the project. One volunteer, who had a disabled family member, chose to pioneer disability access because he felt passionately about it, while volunteers around the world who spoke under-represented languages seized the opportunity to preserve the integrity of their language by translating content. Consequently every new Firefox release is available at launch in more than 75 languages. As long as the initiatives align with the Mozilla philosophy, the organization chooses to make it easier for people to do what they want with the brand. A similar philosophy has also been adopted for marketing the Mozilla brand where a community of marketing professionals and enthusiast consumers helped to construct and implement a marketing campaign, even to the extent of donating money to run a launch campaign in *The New York Times* that featured the names of all those who gave.

If it were the case that Mozilla was simply passing over implementation to volunteers, it could be argued that this is only co-production, not co-creation, but the volunteers have a large say in the overall direction. Dotzler points out that Mozilla gives responsibility to those that do the work. Development modules within the business have owners – people who have authority for the module and vet all changes. Yet even though this is a hierarchical position it is not connected to employment. 'There are many modules which are owned by employees of other companies or are owned by people doing it as a hobby. So every module has an owner and the owners surround themselves with a group of people called peers; they do peer reviews on the

FIGURE 1.1   Firefox Launch Campaign in *The New York Times*. The left hand page features the names of all those individuals who contributed funds for the campaign

code.' Dotzler argues that the whole system works because transparency is a core element of the business philosophy: 'we are as open as we can be.' Mozilla works from the principle that everything that can be put into the public domain from design documents to bug reports, should be. In fact, Mozilla would also put details of employment and contracts out there, if employees would allow it.[13] Mozilla can argue that it has superior products that are widely accessible but the key to its enduring success is its openness to others. Firefox and Thunderbird are co-created by a community of customers and it is the nurturing and support of that community that defines Mozilla's competitive advantage.

Co-creation is empowering

The traditional method for getting close to customers has been to use market research and observational techniques. This approach has the seeming advantage of objectivity because the researcher attempts to remain disengaged from the activities and ideas of participants. Its value is that it can help us gain insight into the attitudes of people towards brands. Yet it is an imperfect tool for generating knowledge about consumer intentions. While research can help us better understand the here and now, if we wish to get closer to customers' likely future behaviour we need a more participative process. With co-creation techniques, customers and other stakeholders do not simply present their opinions but are active creators of a possible future. In co-creation we are less interested in objectivity and rational thought and more in involvement and creativity. This changes the rules of the game. When organizations engage in market research they make no real commitment to participants other than to listen to their views. Consequently there is no shift in the power relationship. The company asks little of participants and gives them no power individually or collectively. It is a casual encounter without obligation for further action. When it comes to co-creation processes, whether it is through face-to-face sessions or online communities, an obligation is created. The level of involvement increases because the organization is not simply asking for a response to a posed question but is asking people to be creative and to help discover new ideas, sometimes in intense work groups and/or long-term communities. For people to be willing to give up their time and to commit themselves to this arrangement, the organization has to be willing to pass over some of its power to the participants. Yet what is the nature of this power? As power flows through individuals the brand ceases to be under the control of the organization and becomes fluid. It is shaped in a moving space of dialogue between the organization and stakeholders, as power flows between them. The organization provides a branded product or service which is used, adapted and discussed by consumers. They create places of discussion, share ideas and influence others. If the organization is attuned to this talk or indeed initiates a forum where ideas can be discussed, it can enter into a conversation. Yet this is only a conversation, a sharing, where there is possibility of movement. If the organization remains rooted in a set way of doing things, it cannot converse. It has to have the will both to listen and to consider the views of others, positively.

From the customer's perspective, conversation may be interesting and stimulate self-discovery and learning, but co-creation implies an even greater commitment. It suggests that people deliver an emotional engagement, involving the totality of their experience, to provide input for an organization. As we saw with Mozilla, people can become involved to extraordinary degrees in the development of ideas, even when they are not employed by an organization. Why would they do this? Often the managerial assumption is that people are driven by monetary reward. This is a version of what is known as extrinsic motivations bias.[14] Yet it is clear from our research that monetary based rewards are of secondary importance to participants. The most important motivation is intrinsic. It is the feeling of being engaged and finding meaning.

Co-creation meets a fundamental need, because 'we cannot bear to live our lives without some sort of content that we can see as constituting a meaning'.[15] While our everyday jobs often fail us in terms of engagement precisely because we are denied the opportunity to contribute creatively, there are communities, events and projects that do provide the opportunity for expressivity. These might be writing schools, painting classes or amateur drama groups, but they can equally be the Adult Friends of Lego (AFOLs), the Porsche Owners Club or the Tata Beverages Online Community. These and numerous other communities enable people to form friendships, discuss ideas with like-minded individuals and to design new concepts. But people will generally only maintain their involvement in these fora if two central conditions are met. First, the subject has to matter to them; they have to care enough about the category or the company to give of themselves. Second, they have to be convinced that their ideas matter to the organization; that they are being listened to, that feedback will be given and good contributions implemented. This involvement generates meaning because people feel they are contributing to the experience of other consumers and simultaneously becoming closer to the organization. Commenting on research on service encounters, Cova and Dalli note, 'The more the customer is involved in the process of service production and delivery, the greater the perceived value and satisfaction. . . Consumers (as individuals and as a group of interacting subjects) become partial employees and employees become partial consumers.'[16] Similarly, in their study of nine brand communities, Schau et al note some emerging perspectives, which include the view that passing control over to customers enhances their sense of engagement and that companies 'derive added brand value by creatively using willing customer resources'.[17]

While empowerment seems a positive move for both the organization and the consumer, we should however be cautious about the implications. The risk the organization runs is that in letting go the brand loses clarity. We will explore this issue more fully in the next chapter, but we can note for now that as people adopt the brand as their own and stretch it in unforeseen ways the concept of the brand can begin to shift in undesired directions and to acquire associations that undermine it. Equally there are dangers for consumers. If consumers give of their time willingly to co-create a product or service, by and large they do so because they find meaning in it. At a basic level, many of the public services and charitable projects that make our world functional and enjoyable are delivered by people giving up their time and creativity for free. When people do this for companies, there is still a benefit for the individual but the gain for the organization will be measured in profits. Whatever is generated by a company-sponsored community becomes the property of the organization. Participants are generally not free to tout around their ideas to other organizations and they do not retain control of their intellectual property. Fair enough, we might say, given that ideas are developed in conjunction with others. A new product or service should not be the property of an individual, for without the community the idea may never have been realized. For critical commentators, co-creation is exploitation and the optimism that surrounds it misplaced.

Not only do consumers give of themselves to create and develop brands but they then pay market prices to consume the products they have added value to. Most consumers do not seem to have reached this critical view themselves, although as the practice of co-creation becomes more widespread those who bring specific professional skills to a community may come to demand more in terms of monetary rewards and rights to intellectual property.

Co-creation involves the organization

There is a swirl of writing on subjects that connect with co-creation, such as crowd sourcing, user-generated content and open-design competitions. All of these areas involve people outside the boundaries of the organization but they do not always encompass empowerment and they do not always directly involve the company itself. The company in some of these cases is either not present or merely a frame to which people add unmediated content. For example, YouTube does allow large numbers of people to generate content but there is no direct interaction between YouTube and the contributor. For co-creation to be realized there needs to be both 'co-' and 'creation'. It must involve the organization, either as the originator of a process or as an active partner in an existing community. And it must allow customers and other interested parties such as employees, entrepreneurs, researchers, experts and investors, a creative role in shaping the future of a product or service. If consumers are required merely to be either a lead tester of a product or an adaptor of a suite of pre-selected choices, it lacks a sense of real creativity where something genuinely new is developed. The underlying factor here is a willingness to impart trust to outsiders, something much easier to achieve if those inside the organization are confident and if outsiders are given an opportunity to be part of the conversation.

Increasingly customers are knowledge providers, idea generators and brand shapers. Through direct interaction they influence the opinions of other stakeholders and help to create a world. The point here is that customers are conversing whether the company is part of the conversation or not. Von Hippel (2006) writes in *Democratizing Innovation* that much innovation is created by users who are just trying to solve immediate problems or to enhance performance. Citing examples from such areas as construction and mountain biking, he shows how people talk, discuss ideas informally and create working prototypes which are then sometimes commercialized once companies appreciate their potential. However, this move from tacit to explicit knowledge does not always occur and some inventions remain temporary and unshared. To increase the chance of spotting or nurturing customers' good ideas, organizations need spaces to interact. In the past these spaces could be physical events such as fairs or workshops that brought together customers and organizational members, or correspondence. The

Internet has changed the dynamic of the exchange by increasing the volume and speed of interaction and the opportunity for the respective parties to become part of each other's networks.

How LEGO learned to share

A much cited example of interaction is LEGO. Hatch and Schultz describe how the LEGO Group embarked accidentally on a voyage of co-creation. When the company launched a new product featuring programmable bricks in 1998 called Mindstorms it was only a matter of hours before the software was hacked and shared. While the initial thought was to take legal action, cool heads prevailed and LEGO decided to give their users a right to hack – something that was positively received by the enthusiasts who made up the LEGO brand community. As a result of this initial contact, LEGO began to be better connected to this core segment of its customer base (Mindstorms is the all-time best selling LEGO product): 'by monitoring various websites and later in engaging in online dialogue and attending AFOL-organized events, top LEGO managers discovered that many AFOLs were eager to engage with the company – they soon began to realize the value of this engagement for the LEGO brand.'[18] When it came to the second generation of Mindstorms, known as NXT, much of the development work was done by four AFOLs who gave their time and creativity to design the new product. While the initial serendipitous event was not initiated by LEGO, the company had the sense to join the conversation that was taking place in one of the existing brand communities. Since realizing the potential of engagement, LEGO has nurtured its community contacts, inviting fans to co-create other products and recruiting ambassadors from among fan brand communities to work in LEGO innovation facilities.

Conclusion

Our cultures have become participatory. The distance that once existed between organizations and customers has been reduced and the authority of experts has diminished. As individuals, we no longer automatically accept the passivity that was once expected of us and instead we sometimes choose to be active participants by defining the relationship that we have with brands and by attempting to influence other stakeholders and the organization itself. This empowers us to be the co-creators of value – a role that satisfies our desire to find meaning in what we do. For the organization, choosing to participate facilitates learning, opens a window to the future and reduces risk. But it only does this when the organization decides to be an authentic conversationalist. In other words, when it approaches the opportunity for dialogue with an open mind and a willingness to adapt its position; to act its way into understanding. This is partly about mechanisms, but it is much more to do with the culture of the organization and whether it is capable of change.

Notes

1 Anderson, Chris. 'Film School: why online video is more powerful than you think.' *Wired* 19.01.11 p 115

2 Johnson, S (2010) *Where Good Ideas Come From: The Natural History of Innovation.* Allen Lane, London p 228

3 Catmull, Ed (2008) 'How Pixar Fosters Collective Creativity.' *Harvard Business Review* 86(9) p 66

4 Über die allmähliche Verfertigung der Gedanken beim Reden

5 Amabile, T M and Khaire, M (2008) 'Creativity and the Role of the Leader.' *Harvard Business Review* 86(10) pp 100–09

6 Porter, R (2000) *Enlightenment: Britain and the Creation of the Modern World.* Allen Lane, The Penguin Press, London

7 In their book on Technology and Innovation, Dodgson, Gann and Salter's list of the major analytical approaches to innovation does not feature anything specific about brand, although it does feature 'market pull', citing Myers and Maquis (1969) and von Hippel (1988). Dodgson, M, Gann, D and Salter, A (2005) *Think, Play, Do: Technology, Innovation and Organization.* Oxford University Press, Oxford p 169

8 Ekvall, G (1997) 'Organizational Conditions and Levels of Creativity.' *Creative Management and Development (3rd edition)*, ed. J Henry, Sage Publications, London p 135

9 Gabor, A (2009) 'The Promise (and Perils) of Open Collaboration.' *Strategy+Business.* 56

10 Baker, A C, Jensen P J, Kolb D A (2005) 'Conversation as Learning Experience.' *Management Learning* 36(4) p 421

11 These include Groonroos (2000), Prahalad and Ramaswamy (2004), Vargo and Lusch (2004), Curtis *et al* (2009), Ramaswamy and Gouillart (2010)

12 Friedrich, R, Peterson, M and Koster, A (2011) 'The Rise of Generation C: How to prepare for the Connected Generation's transformation of the consumer and business landscape.' *Strategy+Business,* February 22, 2011, Issue 62

13 Tim Kitchin in 'Living with Translucency, Preparing for Transparency', charts the way organizations are evolving from an opaque past, where as much as possible was hidden away, to a translucent present, where information is selectively open, to an emerging transparent future, already practised by some, where the boundaries are largely removed 'to create and share trustworthiness'. Kitchin, T (2009) 'Living with Translucency, Preparing for Transparency.' *Journal of the Medinge Group,* vol. 3

14 This is the managerial assumption noted in a 2003 study by Chip Heath at Stanford University, that managers assume employees are primarily motivated by extrinsic rewards, such as pay and conditions, and less by intrinsics, such as the job itself and the ability to contribute to the organization. This is known as extrinsic motivations bias because, while managers believe it to be true, research consistently shows that employees are motivated by intrinsics; by a real desire to do important (as they see it) work. We see similar evidence here with co-creation, particularly in the responses to the motivational issue in the Brand Together community.

15 Svendsen, L (2005) *A Philosophy of Boredom.* (Kjedsomhetens filosofi, 1999: Universitetsforlaget, Oslo) Trans. John Irons, Reaktion Books, London, p 30

16 Cova, B and Dalli, D (2009) 'Working Consumers: The Next Step in Marketing Theory.' *Marketing Theory* 9(3) p 319

17 Schau, H, Jensen, M, Albert M Jr and Arnould, E J (2009) 'How Brand Community Practices Create Value.' *Journal of Marketing,* 73(5) pp 30–51

18 Hatch, M-J and Schultz, M (2010) 'Toward a Theory of Brand Co-Creation with Implications for Brand Governance.' *Journal of Brand Management* 17(8) pp 590–604

A brand of innovation

02

- The brand as innovation framework
  - Orange, Virgin and BMW: brands at work
- Co-creation changes the brand
  - How Patagonia's brand influences its decisions
- Conclusion

'You could say that we are like porridge. First we're like small oat flakes – small, dry, fragile, alone. But then we're cooked with the other oat flakes and become soft. We join so that one flake can't be told apart from another. . . So we are no longer small and isolated but we have become warm, soft, and joined together. Part of something bigger than ourselves. Sometimes life feels like an enormous porridge, don't you think?'[1] **GÖRAN'S SPEECH IN THE FILM** *TOGETHER*

In the literature on innovation generally and co-creation specifically, branding rarely gets a mention.[2] This seems surprising, for the brand both creates a frame for innovation and evolves as a result of innovations by consumers and other stakeholders. The brand is, in this perspective, a fundamental ingredient of co-creation. The barrier to understanding brand in this way may be due to misconceptions about the terminology. Some people think a brand is a logo or advertising or the packaging of a product or service. However, the way we see brand is as a stakeholder experience – the result of hearing about, buying and using something that influences future intentions. We buy a Blackberry, eat at McDonalds', shop with Amazon and donate money to WWF because these choices create a relevant experience that aligns with who we are and how we want to be seen. When managers, consumers and other stakeholders take part in co-creation events and communities they bring their perceptions of a brand with them. It influences how they create and evaluate ideas. In particular the brand provides an important filtering mechanism in determining which ideas to progress and which to discard. In turn as ideas from co-creation are implemented, they help to evolve the brand and its meaning for people.

The idea of the brand as ever-evolving seems strange to some. Certainly traditional descriptions of the brand have tended to see it as static, communication-driven and only focused on consumers. In 1998, Ries and Ries wrote that 'markets may change, but brands shouldn't',[3] – an odd idea that somehow suggests that brands are separate from the markets they serve. If markets change then so must brands. The fact that consumers buy and use brands and share their experiences with others implies a constant state of change. The Ries and Ries perspective looks at the world from the company's point of view and seeks somehow to control the brand. This static picture of brands links back to the idea that marketing communications is the prime determinant of a brand's image. In some instances it may be, but the prevalence of services in OECD countries, the emergence of the idea of a services-dominant logic that argues the brand is co-created with consumers and the concept of the experience economy have shifted branding away from communications to personal interaction; from making promises to keeping them; from something run by the marketing department to an organization-wide operating principle. In this perspective, branding is about people. It is the individuals inside the organization who listen to, connect with and deliver service to stakeholders and it is individual stakeholders who use and take part in a dialogue about the brand. As Figure 2.1 shows, the brand is created in a space of dialogue that is forever in movement as the organization and individuals interact.

Also, individuals interact with other organizations that provide services or distribution and with other individuals. It is the combination of these conversations that creates a set of perceptions. In this model we should also note two further elements. First the model should be seen from above (not read from left to right), which means the organization does not deliver a brand to the individual. Rather, the organization and the individual are already connected. As Heidegger argues, when we encounter something we already have an understanding of it because we are part of the same world.[4] Second, one of the large circles is labelled 'individual'. This is not an ideal term because it somehow suggests a separateness from other individuals. Yet it is designed to emphasize that we can have opinions without buying. In other words we can have views of brands and be quite forceful in our willingness to share them with others, without ever having been a consumer. Overall the model suggests we need an organic, fluid view of brands. The organization may make a promise for its corporate, service or product brand and it may deliver on that promise, but the brand itself is negotiated

FIGURE 2.1   A co-creative brand model

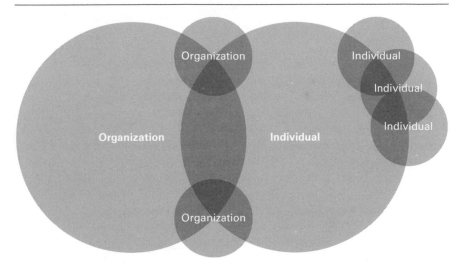

SOURCE Ind and Iglesias 2009

in an ebbing and flowing space that is subject to a wide variety of influences moving increasingly beyond the control of the organization.

The brand as innovation framework

While we can argue that the organization does not 'own' the brand, it does nonetheless attempt to define the brand ideology. This is the set of ideas that is either implicitly held by organizational members or explicitly stated (and sometimes absorbed into behaviours), that defines what the brand is and what it hopes to become. The ideology, which can be structured at the corporate and the product/service level, tries to absorb myriad influences from both inside and outside the organization in defining an idea that is both rooted in the past and stretches towards the future. It should be real and aspirational. It should understand the specific competencies and the culture of the organization/brand and the needs and wants of stakeholders. Various words are used to explain these ideologies such as mission, vision, principles, philosophy, beliefs, and values. If these words sound elevated and spiritual this is no accident. When we find these types of expression in religious texts they are intended as an expression of transcendence removed from the mundane and everyday. The same is true when they are located in annual reports and brand books. The purpose of such words as 'mission', 'vision' and 'values' is to connect employees to a longer-term, purposeful, yet abstracted, ideal. It is for this very reason that the articulation of these brand ideologies (mission, vision and values) is couched in a language that

Orange's five stated behavioural values

Refreshing

Orange is bright and cheerful. Orange aims to liberate people from the constraints of yesterday's technology, providing them with fair, user-friendly products and services, wherever, whenever and however they want to use them.

Honest

Orange is completely transparent, with clear communications that cut through market confusion.

Straightforward

Orange makes things easier by using simple language and no jargon.

Dynamic

Orange is continually developing new services to make communications even easier.

Friendly

Orange is a brand that you can understand and trust.

is designed to inspire. It is an attempt to convey a higher and future-oriented purpose that touches people's deeper motivations.

Orange, Virgin and BMW: brand ideologies at work

The France Telecom owned brand, Orange, has an ideology that talks about a 'commitment to make the world's digital transformation a simple and useful reality for all'. It then articulates five behavioural values that are designed to guide employees' behaviour and approach to communications.

Similarly the Virgin Group's brands, which stretch across mobile telephony, transportation, travel, financial services, media, music and fitness, are unified by a central belief in 'making a difference', which sounds quite similar to Orange's aspiration. Virgin also has a stated set of values: value for money, quality, innovation, fun and a sense of competitive challenge.

The point here of course is whether these ideas have an impact on the behaviour of people. Do managers make investment decisions based on the ideology? Do communications reflect these commitments, beliefs and values? Do employees understand and use these ideas in their day-to-day work? If the ideologies remain the preserve of a spiritual elite in the organization, then they are unlikely to have much effect. For vision and values to be effective they have to be shared. Values, such as those espoused by

Orange and Virgin, are hard to dislike. They are positive, desirable and energizing. If we took Orange's values and ascribed them to a person, we would find that individual likeable and probably engaging. They might also sound too good to be true. So the point we should remind ourselves about with these ideologies, is that while they should be rooted in practice, they are also idealized. They describe how we should behave.[5] Negatively we might see them as manipulative in that they encourage people to deny their individuality and conform to a set of expectations, but positively we can see them as providing an opportunity for individuals to find meaning in their working lives.

When it comes to innovation we might ask what sort of role does the brand ideology play? Is it used to guide thinking and evaluate outputs? Most descriptions from innovation literature don't shed much light because they don't use the terminology of brand or vision and values. However, we would argue that the brand ideology should be used actively in innovation. If the ideology is built on the identity of the organization and the core tenets of the culture, it is an encapsulation of what makes a company unique.

Equally from a stakeholder perspective, the ideology, as expressed in actions and communications, creates a distinctive image for the brand. The image then helps to define the brand scope – what the brand can offer that is appealing and credible. If Orange, for example, were to offer a product that was complicated, inaccessible and lacking customer focus, it would clearly not fit into the scope of the brand and it would have a negative impact on the identity as experienced by employees. A useful metaphor to explain this role of the brand is a framed picture and specifically one by the expressionist artist, Howard Hodgkin. A painting of his, such as 'Dinner at Smith Square', 1975–79, has two interesting features that make it appropriate. First, it was painted over a period of several years as Hodgkin revisited his ideas. Second, he also painted on the frame as well as the canvas. If the frame itself is the brand ideology, we can argue it creates a space where people are free to explore the meaning together as over time they interact with the world and the brand evolves. They also have the opportunity to challenge the frame (by painting on it); to explore the limits of freedom by stretching the brand into new arenas.[6] This is important, because while we want focus, we should not become obsessed with purity. As Mary Douglas notes in her anthropological study *Purity and Danger*, purity 'is the enemy of change, of ambiguity and compromise'. It is Douglas's view that rather than avoiding dirt (matter out of place) we should embrace it because it has the potential to fuel creativity and new ways of seeing things.[7]

When we consider the size of the frame of freedom, we need to recognize that it will vary depending on context. In a design company, the frame might be quite broad, whereas for a logistics company it might be quite narrow. The point is, whatever the size of the space the brand creates a specific area where innovation is most effective. Stephan Durach, Head of the Technology Office for BMW in Palo Alto, notes that the ideas they develop for the different marques within the group – Rolls-Royce, BMW and

Mini – are determined by the nature of the target market and the brand idea. So for Rolls-Royce, innovations need to be highly advanced and sophisticated, whereas for Mini there is a stronger emphasis on fashion and being contemporary and fun. BMW focuses on the idea of joy, which is an emotional concept that emphasizes both the orientation towards drivers and the engineering excellence that generates the driving experience. The different positioning of the brands means that innovations are specifically focused in terms of idea generation and in evaluation and implementation.

Similarly for Orange, innovation is driven by the brand. In 2009, Orange developed a brand strategy that had relationship building as its core idea. When thinking through the implications of this in terms of products and services, initially the emphasis was on what was technically possible. Nick Bonney, Insight Director at Orange, says, 'there were loads of options of things we could do, but it didn't feel like we had it centred on what consumers wanted us to do.' Part of the solution to this was to conduct some intensive workshops with customers where they acted as the researchers and the idea generators. The strength of the participants' understanding of the brand, based on past user experiences and communication, meant they were able to focus their ideas so that they met the brief from Orange and fitted into the brand framework.

Co-creation changes the brand

Just as we can argue that the idea of the brand provides a focus for different stakeholders to develop relevant innovations, so we can also argue that the process of exploration and implementation of ideas has an impact back on the brand. This again challenges the idea that brands shouldn't change and instead recognizes the reality of their connectedness to the world, something that Eric S Raymond, referring to open source, likened to a bazaar where there is an opportunity for interaction and adaptation.[8] In a similar way, Henry Chesbrough points out that people often use technology developed by organizations in ways that were never intended, but provided receptivity and iterative loops of learning exist, continued evolution is possible. In Figure 2.2, we can see how the process of co-creation impacts back on the brand. Inside the organization, which is porous and absorbing influences from the outside, the basic elements of the brand are developed.

In a co-creation process there is then some degree of empowerment. The brand owners let go of the brand and allow it to evolve in a participative way which, as we saw in Chapter 1, can either be initiated by the organization or in response to an already existing community. Assuming that the organization is receptive to the influence of external stakeholders, lessons are absorbed, and the brand evolves through further participation.[9] In describing the model we need a starting point, which is possible when the brand is a new start-up, but when the brand is already established the actual starting

FIGURE 2.2 Empowerment and evolution

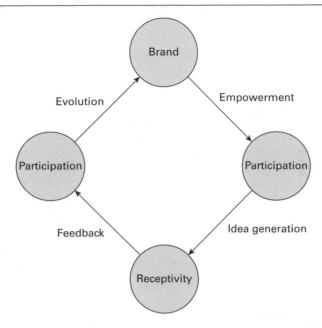

point is problematic because the swirl of influence and adaptation is already in motion. As the organization sets out its brand strategy it is already participating with its stakeholders and learning as it goes along. There is no possible neutral position here. Adaptation goes on all the time.

However, when we suggest there is adaptation, we have to ask what does this mean in practice? Again we should remind ourselves that the meaning of the words used to describe the brand ideology and the meaning or functionality of the brand are subject to change. One of the myths of brand ideologies is that once they are articulated they are somehow fixed. Yet as a community of people use a word to guide their thinking and actions it acquires a specific context for that community. So while we might look at some of the words that Orange uses, such as 'friendly' and 'dynamic', and think any organization could use such values, in fact they have a specific but evolving meaning inside Orange, based on how they guide behaviour, which in this instance has clearly evolved away from a dictionary definition of the words.[10] For example, 'friendly' is co-created by interactions inside and outside the organization. It suggests an organization that encourages close relationships across its business and one that connects with its customers. It suggests a certain tone of voice to communication that is less corporate and more conversational. It implies that there is honesty and clarity and that the company keeps its promises to its stakeholders. It suggests a willingness to listen to customers. At a level below these general principles it directs products such as Magic Numbers (reduced rate calls with friends) and Orange

Wednesdays (offers on cinema tickets), management interaction with Orange Complaints and the use of co-creation to develop new product ideas based around relationships.

As a way of achieving a more precise idea of the intended meaning of its values, Orange explains what it means by such words as 'dynamic' (Orange is continually developing new services to make communications even easier) and 'friendly' (Orange is a brand that you can understand and trust) and by using narratives to illustrate context. However, any sense of finality is elusive. As Michael Anker notes, we never reach an end point in this process, because 'every decision reorganizes the fabric of life, but each move in itself does not lead to a conclusive point of certainty; it leads to a new, uncertain, undecidable, and aporetic space from which once again we must decide and act.'[11] This fluidity can be discomforting, but as the architect, Frank Gehry, demonstrates, it also creates an opportunity to act one's way into deeper meaning. Gehry's approach is to tolerate ambiguity as it develops; to stay in motion rather than reaching towards a conclusion, such that each new phase 'breathes new life into the dream'. Provided one stays open to new possibilities there is the possibility of discovering new and revealing ideas throughout the process.[12]

How Patagonia's brand influences its decisions

Sportswear brand Patagonia is a prime example of a company that is explicit about the ideology of its environmentally focused brand. This is a significant attractor for employees and a guide to action inside the organization. Although the principle of environmentalism goes back some 50 years to the foundation of the company, it was only articulated specifically as part of the mission and values of the business in 1996. If one looks at the history of Patagonia, one can see an emergent idea that develops partly in reaction to events in the external world and partly because of the principles of the founder of the business. Environmentalism as an idea has come to mean something specific for Patagonia:

- Full traceability of all products covering energy consumption involved in making the product, distance travelled, CO_2 emissions, waste produced and water consumption. Positives and negatives are featured on the Patagonia web site.

- Innovative use of materials to create recycled and recyclable products. Principle of reduce (use less), repair (free service), reuse (donate) and recycle (of Patagonia and other brands). All Patagonia products are recyclable.

- Donations to environmental causes. Employees can take time off to work for environmental charities and can also spend time working on the Estancia Valle Chacabuco – a national park supported by a former CEO of Patagonia.

- Demonstrating the success of Patagonia as a business model where profitability is allied to environmentalism and encouraging and guiding other businesses to act likewise.

In describing the Patagonia brand, there is some suggestion of finality, but the meaning of 'environmentalism' or other values such as 'quality' and 'not bound by convention' will continue to evolve as the organization experiments and learns. Indeed Patagonia is an organization that has been visited and written about many times and what is observable is that although the principle of environmentalism has been discussed the way it is interpreted by stakeholders has shifted as ideas have been implemented. This sense of movement in the meaning of the words shows that the brand is not simply the result of decisions made by managers. It is due to the influence and involvement of friends, customers and other stakeholders in 'the tribe' of interested individuals. For example, there is an active blog in which people share their experiences of climbing, skiing, canoeing and other active sports as well as environmental issues. There is ongoing feedback in Patagonia stores where customers tell staff about their experiences. Narratives are absorbed into marketing communications and shared again through photographs and stories of customers wearing Patagonia products. There is an ongoing face-to-face dialogue between active sports people with employees, who also tend to be active sports people themselves. Even the environmental policy that is so core to Patagonia was stimulated by a campaigner who presented himself to the company in 1973 as the representative of the 'Friends of the Ventura River' (even though at the time he was the only friend).

It is both the everyday and exceptional experiences of different stakeholders that leads to learning as the sense of the brand evolves. Patagonia's CEO, Casey Sheahan, observes that customers move from being occasional purchasers to 'cheerleaders – people who love the brand so much that they do the marketing for us.' During the course of their evolution to advocates for the brand, they become closer to the organization, more emotionally connected and more directly influential of its policies and actions. At the same time external stakeholders are evolving in their brand beliefs, so too do organizational members, provided they have the ability to sense and learn. For example, the encounters that sales staff working in a retail shop have will only impact on the brand if they appreciate the significance of conversations with customers and have the opportunity to share what they hear. Inevitably in this process they will forget some things and filter out others that may have been important, but whether they capture and share good ideas will depend on their understanding of the business priorities. In the case of Patagonia, managers try to provide this focus by spending time with each employee and training them on the values by referring to the product attributes and using stories that illustrate the customer experience. Equally, as employees meet and talk to customers they acquire knowledge which can feed back into the culture and help to shape the future evolution of the brand as ideas are incorporated into products.

CASE STUDY   Dr Henrik Sjödin discusses
the nature of a brand promise

Where lies the promised land

Much of the everyday innovation that goes on in the marketplace does not
register on emotional seismographs. Product upgrades, service improvements and new
communications are launched without great involvement from consumers. Some of them
survive, many of them do not. Disappointments are quietly buried and forgotten. New
efforts are devised and cautiously rolled out. Brands change slowly, through reform rather
than revolution.

Once in a while, attempts at innovation cause a bit more drama. I am particularly
intrigued by innovation efforts that become controversial for reasons beyond product
performance. I think that these episodes can be useful to explore the conditions of contemporary brand development. They illuminate what it means to push boundaries. They
capture how the promises that people associate with brands matter to innovation efforts.

The re-design of promises

What do Tropicana, Starbucks, and Gap have in common? Yes, they are all very popular
brands, loved by millions of people. They are also brands that in recent years made seemingly mundane decisions that turned out to be controversial among their very own fans.

In 2009, Tropicana changed the packaging design of their juice cartons. PepsiCo,
which owns Tropicana, had wanted to update the look of the juice and commissioned a
well-known design agency to change the styling. The agency did away with several long-
standing design elements and the result differed markedly from the original Tropicana
packaging. When the new cartons hit the shelves PepsiCo soon heard from concerned
and annoyed customers. Before long they backtracked. Sacrificing efforts spent on advertising the new look of Tropicana, the company decided to return to the original packaging.

As reported in *The New York Times*, February 22 2009, it was not the volume of the
outcries that led to the corporate change of heart. Neil Campbell, president at Tropicana
North America, said 'it was a fraction of a percent of the people who buy the product.'
Rather, the criticism is being heeded because it came, he said in a telephone interview on
Friday, from some of 'our most loyal consumers.' 'We underestimated the deep emotional
bond' they had with the original packaging, he added. 'Those consumers are very important to us, so we responded.'

To what extent the real reason behind the reversal had to do with disappointing sales
might remain an open question; the explanation offered by the company is interesting in
its own right.

In 2010, fashion retailer Gap replaced their classic white-text-on-blue-plate logo with
a new design. Aiming for a more contemporary look, Gap wished to unveil a logo that
reflected efforts to make stores and products more up-to-date and attractive in the current market. What they got was a debacle. First their new logo was mocked and taunted
in social media. Traditional media was not slow in picking up on the controversy, further
amplifying the protests by sceptical fans of the brand. In a crowdsourcing-fashion attempt

to appease critics, Gap then responded by inviting all interested to submit their own alternative designs. This did not work either. Within days the company announced that it would cancel plans to change the logo. Reported on FT.com, October 12 2010, Marka Hansen, head of Gap in North America, explained that 'all roads were leading us back to the blue box' and she elaborated:

> We are clear that we did not go about this in the right way. We recognise that we missed the opportunity to engage with the online community. This wasn't the right project at the right time for crowd sourcing. There may be a time to evolve our logo, but if and when that time comes we'll handle it in a different way.

Finally, in 2011, Starbucks joined Tropicana and Gap in this trio of loved brands having faced the mixed blessing of passionate consumers. Again, design was the issue. Perhaps acting on ambitions to offer more than coffee or to expand further internationally, Starbucks zoomed in on their famous Siren figure framed in a green circle and took away 'Starbucks Coffee' from its logo entirely. Soon enough Facebook and Twitter reverberated with critical comments. However, unlike their two design-changing peers, Starbucks stood their ground. Maybe they were better prepared for the reactions; maybe they were just more self-confident.

An interesting thing about these initiatives from Tropicana, Gap, and Starbucks is that they upset customers even though they do not seem to alter the brand promise in any fundamental way. The juice would remain the same. You would still be able to buy the same jeans in the same stores. Coffee would be brewed just as before. Perhaps this is a good reason to be mindful of how we think about a notion such as brand promise. The long-established branding metaphor of a promise suggests that the company commits to something that customers can rely on. The conundrum is that it is not necessarily clear exactly what that commitment really is. The social contract will always be under-specified.

The examples illustrate how it is not in the power of marketers to single-handedly decide, and for that matter perhaps not even to distinguish for themselves, what is or is not covered by the promises they have given. Tropicana, Gap, and Starbucks now know that design counts as an implicit but important part of their promises. At least two of the three spent energy and resources that they might wish they had spent elsewhere.

A time-machine thought-experiment

In the research leading up to my dissertation, I took interest in the launch of the Porsche Cayenne. The Porsche version of a sports utility vehicle was introduced in 2002 but announced some 4-5 years before that. At that time the idea of a Porsche deviating from a traditional sports car was wildly unpopular among parts of their enthusiast customer base. As these fans understood the 'innovation', it would just contradict so many things the brand should stand for. Their judgement was both a moral ruling, framing the initiative as a sell-out, and a risk assessment, identifying it as a threat to the brand and their relationship to it.

Again, one might argue that the Cayenne did not really change anything for existing customers of Porsche. Nobody was about to tinker with cars that the enthusiasts already owned; nothing would change in service agreements. What seemed to be at stake, however, was a largely implicit part of the promise. This part had to do with what Porsche was supposed to be in the future, what they would devote resources to, and their reliability in helping customers to desired identities and images of themselves.

Porsche management went ahead and built the Cayenne anyway. In many ways, it became a smash hit. It soon became the best-selling Porsche model and is sometimes credited with saving the company. The case illustrates how vantage points differ. Porsche management analyzed the situation differently from anxious loyalists, based on different input. They were ready to alienate part of their customer base to gain something they deemed necessary. The company then built a high-performance car that was well-received by motor journalists and a comparatively broad group of prospects. In financial terms, it paid off.

Were Porsche managers right to ignore the hardcore protesters? Shareholders might say yes. If the Cayenne really saved the company, perhaps even the then-critics could admit that it was right to renegotiate the brand promise. On the other hand, some of them might retort that there could have been other, less compromising, paths to success. There is always room for debate. Perhaps a more interesting question is this: would it even have been built today? Would Porsche have been able to ignore their critics even if they wanted to, had the Cayenne been planned a decade later? Remember that at the turn of the millennium, social media was certainly not the established phenomenon that it is today. Aficionados could vent frustration in enthusiast forums, but did not have a thriving blog culture, Facebook or Twitter, where their protests could pick up momentum with a more mainstream audience. New channels and patterns of behaviour have enhanced the power of snowballing campaigns. Could annoyed Porsche lovers have achieved what annoyed fans of Tropicana and Gap did? Could they have scared management into not pursuing the plans for the Cayenne?

I am not sure about the answer. However, I am pretty sure that Porsche managers would have had to think differently about the whole process. A passive approach would most likely be doomed. It would be obvious that there would be more at stake than the purchasing power of a concerned clique. Vocal enthusiasts could take charge of the process. Using social media, they could shape the perceptions of important stakeholders and mainstream markets. To get Cayenne approved, management would need to manage renegotiations for a new Porsche promise to fit the innovation. Effectively, they would have to figure out ways to liaise, listen, and lead.

Liaising

Today's innovators need to figure out how to build working relationships with customers who feel that they too have a stake in the business. For some, a comprehensive crowd-sourcing platform makes sense, others are fine with a development blog, while still others meet their community face-to-face. The tools should fit the needs. I think the important point is that they reach out and are willing to engage.

Listening

To renew a brand promise, innovators need to figure out interests, priorities, and opportunities for common ground early on. They can avoid a great deal of trouble just by being attentive to how people view the current brand promise in its totality. The ambition to learn more about the lives of customers and hear about their worries can fuel both innovation and communication. Allowing customers a creative role can then build both confidence and energy. It can help initiate the right innovation efforts and keep them on the right track. A series of events where customers, product development people and managers work together on new ideas could be one example of how to jointly explore the meaning and versatility of a brand promise. Soliciting feedback does not mean surrendering a unique point of view but offers clues on effective next steps—whether they take a project in a new direction or improve support for staying on course. It puts current reasoning to the test and generates stronger arguments going forward.

Leading

Although contemporary innovators should understand their limits in determining the fate of brands, they have not lost their ability to shape opinion. I think it is a mistake to confuse the need to listen with abdication. Managers still have the power to make informed judgements. They still have the means to influence people to see things they would not otherwise see. However, like all opinion-leaders, they need to plant ideas for growth. They need to have a vision and be savvy about how to establish and adapt it through feedback.

A final thought on promising

A promise is a tricky thing. When does a promisor have the right to break or revise one? When promisees say it is okay? If we take the metaphor of a promise seriously in branding, this is what liaising, listening, and leading would aim for.

There is another view that promisors can change their mind because the promise was temporary, dynamic, and elastic. Maybe this is where more brands are headed? Innovation becomes less of a project and more of a process. Companies and customers might agree on a 'constant beta version' mindset. Change comes as no surprise, and customers grant managers some latitude in return for responsiveness and opportunities to contribute.

Henrik Sjödin, PhD
Stockholm School of Economics Institute for Research

Conclusion

The ideology of a brand creates a framework for innovation. It sets out a certain set of ideas that provide a focus for new products and services that make it more relevant for one company to develop something than another. Whether the ideology is actively used inside the organization will determine the coherence of the brand. If the ideology is weak the challenge will be digression and deviation. Even though the ideology is normally structured to give guidance, we should at the same time recognize that brands are fluid entities that are shaped by the interaction between organizational members and external stakeholders. They evolve because of the experiences and resulting expectations of people as they buy, use, adapt, discuss and interact with the brand and the absorption of those experiences by employees who in turn can use that knowledge to re-structure and re-present the brand. In this line of thought, co-creation is intimately connected to the brand. It is the brand ideology that shapes co-creation processes both by setting a direction for creativity and by providing a means of evaluating ideas generated in collective contexts. On the other hand the actions of customers and other stakeholders taken together with those of the company help to develop the meaning of the brand ideology.

Notes

1 From the 2000 Lukas Moodysson film, *Tillsammans (Together)*

2 Payne, A, Storbacka, K, Frow, P and Knox, S (2009) 'Co-Creating Brands: Diagnosing and Designing the Relationship Experience.' *Journal of Business Research* **62** pp 379–89

3 Ries, A and Ries, L (1998) *The 22 Immutable Laws of Branding: How to Build a Product or Service into a World-Class Brand* p 153, Harper Business, New York

4 Heidegger, M (1962) *Being and Time.* (Sein und Zeit, Max Niemeyer Verlag, Tübingen, 1927) Trans. John Macquarrie and Edward Robinson, Blackwell, Oxford

5 In Charles Bukowski's novel *Post Office* (1971), which clearly mirrors Bukowski's own life, a postal worker called Henry Chinaski challenges the ideology of the US Post Office given on the opening page of the book, espousing a set of ideals that employees should embrace, such as 'unwavering integrity', 'complete devotion', the 'highest moral principles' and acting with 'honor and integrity worthy of the public trust'. Chinaski does not respect those he works with and rejects the idea of devotion. Instead he continually challenges the ideology. After working as a mail carrier for three years and then for 12 years as a mail sorter, just like Bukowski, Chinaski then leaves to write a novel.

6 One of the expert reviewers of *Brand Together*, Christof Zürn points out that the jazz musician Miles Davis is an interesting example of an organic brand. The musicians that worked with him and challenged him became a part of the Miles Davis brand. Davis changed his music radically over time (always together with excellent musicians). He was sometimes criticized for taking new directions, but he always stayed true to his beliefs. Even some of the musicians he worked with did not really understand what he was doing, or what he wanted, but they trusted and respected him to create something special.

7 Douglas, M (2002) *Purity and Danger.* (Routledge and Kegan Paul, 1966), Routledge Classics, London

8 Raymond, E S (1999) *The Cathedral and the Bazaar: Musings on Linux and Open Source by an Accidental Revolutionary.* O'Reilly Sebastopol, California

9 Vargo, S L and Lusch, R F (2004) 'Evolving to a New Dominant Logic for Marketing.' *Journal of Marketing* **68** pp 1–17

10 Dictionary.com describes 'dynamic' as pertaining to or characterized by energy or effective action; vigorously active or forceful; energetic; and 'friendly' as characteristic of or befitting a friend; showing friendship: a friendly greeting.

11 Anker, M (2009) *The Ethics of Uncertainty: Aporetic Openings.* Atropos Press, New York p 61

12 Weick, K E (2003) 'Organizational Design and the Gehry Experience.' *Journal of Management Enquiry* **12**(1) pp 93–97

Co-creation and the organization

03

- The rejectors
  - Invention, not innovation at PARC
  - Consumer-focused innovation at Electrolux
  - Apple's focus on experience
- The experimenters
  - Barclays and Dragons' Den
- The enthusiasts
  - Intuit's commitment to innovation
- Conclusion

'A fundamental element of human nature is the need for creative work, for creative enquiry, for free creation.'[1]
NOAM CHOMSKY

The linguist and philosopher, Noam Chomsky, has long been an advocate of the need to create the opportunity for people to express their creativity because, as he sees it, creativity is core to our being and is too often denied us. One of the virtues of co-creation is that it provides an arena for creative expression. From a different perspective leaders also see the vital importance of creativity. In IBM's CEOs study (2010), the authors saw the importance of creative thinking as a means to revitalize strategies and adapt them to new contexts. Whereas once there was a strong belief among managers in a planned approach to strategy, there is a growing commitment to the idea of emergence – of 'continuously re-conceiving' strategies. The implication of this is that the real currency inside leading organizations is fresh ideas that 'are intended to disrupt the status quo'. Alongside this focus is a simultaneous recognition of the need to become closer to customers. AG Lafley, the former CEO of P&G, argued in an interview that you need to get so close to customers that you can understand their needs and wants, even when they can't articulate them themselves. Part of Lafley's argument is that you have to work at becoming more open and receptive if you want to be innovative. In the case of P&G this has become an organization-wide commitment – a quest to ingrain customer-centricity into the culture. This emphasis is important, for while the Internet and the emergence of social media is a facilitator of customer closeness, it is not a prerequisite. Indeed, while the online world does enable the organization and the individual to become close, it also has the potential to increase the distance. We no longer need to seek out the organization for dialogue or answers to questions but rather we can talk to friends, community members and mediators that exist beyond the boundaries – and perhaps influence – of the organization. For closeness to be realized we need to be able to think beyond the tools and focus on the relevance of the dialogue and the opportunity to enable creativity.

In this chapter, we will explore different organizational approaches to co-creativity. While most leading organizations recognize the importance of creativity in strategy development, new product and process development and innovation implementation, their willingness to engage in co-creation varies. Some organizations adopt Henry Ford's view of consumer input and reject co-creation, preferring to rely on their own observations and expertise to innovate. Others are experimenters. They tend to see co-creation as an alternative to traditional research techniques or internal engagement processes and are using it to test how customers and employees can contribute to innovation. Some are working towards making co-creation a way of life involving all their stakeholders. Each of these attitudes towards innovation has its own particular challenges and we will explore each in turn, illustrating them through examples.

The rejectors

There is a view of innovation which believes in the sanctity of expertise and rejects the active involvement of customers or other stakeholders. This perspective works on the premise that the professional and expert skills of the people inside the organization are better placed to create new products and services than external parties who lack the requisite knowledge and experience. Sometimes this belief is pervasive because of deeply rooted cultures that have enjoyed past success from a closed model and invention not innovation – the distinction being that invention is the creation of something new without reference to its potential commercialization, whereas innovation additionally incorporates customer acceptance and market performance.[2] Sometimes it is because organizations have discovered methods other than co-creation for generating insight into customers' attitudes and behaviour. The former belief is becoming increasingly difficult to sustain but it can be hard for some organizations to change because they are trapped by inward-looking cultures where invention, often engineering- or technology-led, dominates and both the customer and their own marketing department are peripheral. These are places where people delight in the pursuit of excellence for its own ends and only then look up and wonder who might buy what they have created.

Invention, not innovation at PARC

One of the criticisms of Xerox's inventive Palo Alto Research Center (PARC) is that, while it generated many of the ideas that created the modern computing industry, it also suffered from a want of customer orientation. Chesbrough notes, 'customers often did not know what to make of a new technology they were seeing at PARC.[3] They might be intrigued by its technical dimensions but have no sense of how to make use of it. Xerox's own sales force similarly might struggle to find a value proposition for a fledgling technology.'[4] PARC was staffed by a formidable cadre of scientists and technologists who brought tremendous intellectual capacity to the organization, but no real focus on customers. As a consequence, some of the inventions that came out of PARC never did find a real use while some meandered to eventual success by stumbling on something of value. PARC is not atypical in this respect. There are many examples of organizations floundering before attaining clarity. Probably the most famous is the way Honda bumbled its way to success with its range of mopeds in the US through a combination of luck and accident.

PARC and some of the companies that broke away from it, such as 3com and Adobe, had clever technologies, but they were inventing in a vacuum away from the market. Without significant input from those who might use, distribute or license a technology, they struggled to determine likely consumer acceptance and viable business models, especially when they were dealing with a rapidly changing industry where the standards were still in the process of being defined. For example, at the beginning Adobe had to sense and guess its way to realizing its potential. It found out what worked by doing, learning and adapting, which sounds rather like co-creation. And in a sense it is, but PARC and its protégés only began to co-create right at the end of the process after they had made several wrong turns. Ideally, co-creation involves stakeholders earlier in the process when questions and possibilities are still open. Then people can give input that can shape a product and reduce risk through involvement in prototyping and product testing.

Consumer-focused innovation at Electrolux

An example of an organization that has made this transition is Electrolux, the Swedish home appliance manufacturer. Electrolux, founded in 1919 is the second largest home appliances company in the world, and until

Whirlpool's acquisition of Maytag in 2006, was the largest. The company's success was rooted in invention and it was a strongly engineering-led culture until the early 2000s. This was a viable approach when the main basis of competition was product performance and price, but as consumers became more demanding, not least because of their interactions with other technologies, and more aesthetically aware, a different approach became necessary. It was no longer enough just to make something more powerful or effective, it had to deliver a relevant experience. As a result, Electrolux started to shift its approach to become more consumer-centric and brand focused in its approach to innovation.[5] Head of Design, Henrik Otto, argues that 'you can't afford to do technical innovation internally and then best guess whether it is going to be a success, because the consumer might not be as fascinated with the technical genius of what it is that you have created. . . the product experience is much more accurate and relevant if you start from the angle of specific issues for specific consumers.' Otto additionally points out that you have to create a sense of what the brand stands for through the product experience, its design language and communications, if you are to generate the distinctiveness that can lead to brand loyalty.

The Electrolux perspective is that consumer closeness makes good business sense because it is the primary way to reduce risk. Yet in spite of this orientation Electrolux is not a believer in co-creation. The argument is two-fold. First, consumers may be able to give input on what might be possible in the present, but they lack the reference frame and the knowledge of product development to contribute effectively to what might be viable in 5 or 10 years. Second, there is a sense that if you ask a consumer to identify an issue or a problem, they respond with an answer that concentrates on the effect rather than the underlying cause.

Electrolux's primary means of consumer insight is an observation programme that involves people from different parts of the organization. This helps to generate a sense of identification with consumers and their needs and also a passion for the resulting products. As observation is a continuous process it also helps to ensure that the insight generated is as up-to-date as possible. The principle behind the method is to encourage employees to observe how people really live in their homes without pre-judgement or initially asking questions. After observation, employees question people's behaviour and their motivations and at a later stage after developing prototypes, consumers will be asked for their input as a part of the product refinement. However, consumers will not be required to actively co-create the product, which is seen as the domain of the product developers and designers. It is their expert task to interpret the observations and to define direction.

The Ergorapido vacuum cleaner provides an apt example of the method. Electrolux found that when they notified a family with young children that they would visit and observe their use of appliances, the vacuum cleaner would always be in a cupboard, whereas if the visit was spontaneous the vacuum cleaner would be out because of the continuous requirement for instant cleaning. The insight was that large traditional vacuum cleaners were not well suited for everyday cleaning and that their lack of aesthetic appeal precluded their display when visitors were coming. The result was a brief to develop a product that catered for instant cleaning and looked cool enough and took up as little space as possible so that people would leave it out all the time. Within Electrolux the product team conceived and prototyped a new product that was then tested back with potential users. The Ergorapido, as it became known, is a chargeable stick vacuum cleaner with a detachable handheld piece that can be used for small cleaning jobs, such as upholstery. Key to its success has been not only the instant cleaning functionality but also the aesthetic appeal of its sleek minimalistic design and the strong use of colour that encourages people to keep it on display in the home. Technologically, there is nothing particularly distinctive about the Ergorapido, but it is clearly positioned for a particular market segment and meets a specific need. We might wonder whether the same success could be achieved by co-creative methods, but it is impossible to know. For Electrolux, consumer closeness is achieved primarily through an ethnographic approach and it seems to have been effective. It helps to remind us that co-creation, while much talked about, is not the only way to innovate.

Apple's focus on experience

Included also in the category of co-creation rejectors is a highly innovative company, Apple. Like Electrolux it prefers to use its internally developed expertise to design and develop new products and experiences. Yet it is still a determinedly customer-oriented business that innovates within the framework of its brand. Apple is well connected to its fan and professional user base and it does use research to generate insights into customer behaviour. Interestingly though, this seems not to be about asking people to suggest what they want, but rather to explore people's whole lives (not just what they do as consumers at the point of purchase) and from there to make the imaginative leap to innovation. For example, when Apple developed its retail concept with its Genius Bar, where customers could consult with well trained and highly competent 'geniuses', they asked people to describe their best customer service experience. The most frequent mention was the concierge desk in a hotel which is there to provide a service, not to sell something. The take out from this was the idea to create a friendly, non-selling place within the retail experience where you could talk to knowledgeable people without feeling any pressure to buy.[6] Not only did the solution meet customers' deeper needs for reassurance when buying and using technology, but it also clearly aligned with the brand vision to 'enrich lives'. Indeed the core strength of the Apple approach has been its long-term recognition of the services-dominant logic of marketing, the principle that all products are in reality co-created services, because it is the long-term usage experience of the product that determines the relationship between the organization and the customer.

The success of innovation at Apple has long been rooted in its people-centric approach; an emphasis on product use rather than the transaction; on human–machine interaction rather than the virtues of the technology itself. Steve Jobs has said of Apple (and also Pixar, which he helped to establish) that 'they both deliver a product that has immense technology unerpinnings and yet they both strive to say you don't need to know anything about this technology in order to use it.'[7] Go back to the launch of the Macintosh in 1984 and there are some telling points that demonstrate the view that less is more. The launch advertisement headline reads: 'Introducing Macintosh. For the rest of us.' The claim of the advertisement is that for the first time engineers have focused on people not expert users. 'Since computers are so smart, wouldn't it make more sense to teach computers about people, instead of teaching people about computers?' While allowing for some hyperbole, the headline does reflect a commitment to the customer experience which has guided Apple's approach to innovation. Jobs argues there is no innovation method at the company, but what does emerge from the company's approach is a clearly focused innovation culture that is driven by deep-rooted insight into people's behaviour and a willingness to 'think different'.

The experimenters

The idea of experimenting with co-creation as a means of generating user insight has only become mainstream in recent years. Yet it has been practiced in different forms for much longer. For example, what was known as Cooperative Design, which developed in Scandinavia in the 1970s, centred around the design and use of technology at work and involved users in making an active contribution to computer applications in development. Often trade unions also took part in the process. The thinking behind Cooperative Design was to provide some empowerment to workers and to generate their active input. One of the important elements of the process was the continuous use of prototypes as a mechanism to bring sometimes abstract ideas to life and to generate feedback and suggestions. Bødker and Grønbæk argued that, 'We see prototyping with active user involvement as a way of overcoming some of the problems that current approaches have with developing computer applications that fit the actual needs of the users.'[8] Subsequently the idea of prototyping was extended to make it explicitly more democratic. Grønbæk *et al*, described an approach defined as Cooperative Experimental System Development (CESD).[9] This was similar to Cooperative Design and was characterized specifically by its focus on: 'active user involvement throughout the *entire* development process; prototyping experiments *closely coupled* to work-situations and use-scenarios; *transforming results* from early cooperative analysis/design to targeted object oriented design, specification, and realization; and design for *tailorability*.' The use of prototypes has remained a key element in the co-creation process. Taking part in creating prototypes helps users to formulate and structure their ideas, especially when they need to drill down into the meaning of hard-to-pin-down concepts such as quality or service and to make the intangible more tangible. For example, the airline Etihad has involved its customers from around the world to generate the broad concepts and prototypes for the cabin interiors for its Airbus A380 planes.

Another strand of co-creation experimentation has developed out of existing brand communities. While organizations were taking the initiative to involve users in co-creating software, consumers were forming their own communities. As one of the facets of brands is their ability to help define a sense of self-identity, it should not be surprising that communities have formed around brands. The sense of a shared enthusiasm for a brand has driven people to sometimes ignore their immediate neighbours in a search for community and instead focus on those with a similar consumption experience. Muniz and O'Guinn documented such brands as Saab, Ford and Apple that had the power to bring consumers together to discuss ideas and experiences.[10] Such communities created an opportunity for meaning-making and thereby deepened the sense of connectivity to the brand. Sometimes brand owners, such as Saab, provided material and support for these communities, but it has only been with the growth of Internet access that it has become viable for companies to begin testing out how they could really connect with and engage credibly with community members.

Social media is also playing a growing role in enabling brands and consumers to connect better with each other. For example, British fashion and beauty weekly magazine *more!*, which has a circulation of around 188,265, used Facebook and their 105,000 fans as a tool to co-create a special edition of the magazine. *more!* is a brand that already has very high levels of interactivity because of the continuous exchange of ideas, tips, confidences and opinions between Facebook fans and magazine staff. The supportive culture that has developed on the Facebook page drives participation and, on occasion, a sense of influence over the magazine's content. For the co-creation issue, *more!* is the first publication to open up and invite readers and Facebook fans to participate on editorial direction, to vote on the cover star, to edit pictures for features and to appear as models in the fashion pages and much more. Additionally, five 'superfans' applied through Facebook for the chance to work on the issue in the office for the day. *more!* collaborated with the five readers, between 20–22 years, who wrote copy, attended news meetings, approved layouts and chose headlines. And even lunched with the editor! The process generated over 19,000 wall posts and comments and 62,359 visits to the page during the week alone. Perhaps, just as interesting is the sense of excitement among those that contributed.

Online initiatives such as those undertaken by *more!* have started to make some companies close to customers again, something that had often been lost as companies grew ever larger and more remote. Similarly, customers are more used to the idea of participation both because of the online opportunity and the influence of television. While for many years there have been quiz shows and forms of audience participation on television, since 1999, with the first showing of *Big Brother*, there has been a boom in reality television. The development of programmes involving members of the public in performing tasks, interacting with each other and reflecting on their own behaviour, often in an isolated space, is a form of community-making, albeit one with very specific rules. People get the chance to express themselves in the space they are given, even if the rules of the game limit the potential to influence things in any fundamental way. Nonetheless, as we will see, some of the ideas from reality television have been adapted to the co-creation environment as a way of unlocking new ways of thinking.

Barclays and Dragons' Den

Barclays Bank has been experimenting with co-creation using a face-to-face method of engagement based around the popular reality television format, Dragons' Den (Shark Tank in the US). In the TV programme, which originated in Japan but has since spread round the world, would-be entrepreneurs present their ideas to a team of dragons – the potential investors. The television programme embraces a certain confrontational tone as the entrepreneurs and investors face-off, but while this might make for good television this aspect was not integral to the Barclays use of the concept. Barclays' goal was to try and capture market share in a specific segment: students. In the UK this has been a market dominated by one bank, NatWest, who seem to have the killer promotion in the form of a student railcard. For many years Barclays had used research to validate different aspects of a student account without ever quite generating a breakthrough idea. The view internally was that maybe the incentive itself wasn't that important but neither was it clear what exactly was the key to success. The idea of using the Dragons' Den approach was to see if a more participative method could provide the depth that had been missing from the previous research. Co-creation also seemed to be a better way to look at all of the component parts of the offer and create and test a proposition which was a sum of the parts as opposed to just validating the individual components. George Penman, then Propositions Manager for Students at Barclays, adds, 'there was another part of this which took us down the co-creation route which was that it is not just about the proposition itself, but that it could give us much more insight into the journey that students go on in terms of when they start shopping around for accounts; what their drivers and motivations are for choosing accounts; how we should be communicating with them; and outside of the offer itself, what else could we be doing in the student space to support them.' The method also allowed for a certain degree of adaptability in that Barclays could put an idea in front of students and let them either mould it into something that was more approriate and powerful or reject it. From an initial briefing by Barclays, the students worked in small groups to develop concepts and then they pitched them back to Barclays managers. Penman says that many of the ideas generated linked back to concepts that had been discussed before, but also there were certain things, such as credit cards, that Barclays thought were a compelling part of the offer, but really didn't seem to be important:

> We got some great feedback, well, more than feedback. They specifically articulated the role that the incentive plays in the proposition, which is more than we could have asked for. So their view was that the incentive provides the purpose of convincing students to talk to you . . . once you are in the door and understand the incentive, then it is the details of the account that matter.

Perhaps just as important as the structure of the offer was the tone of communications. It was clear from the students that Barclays was not considered as a student brand. This lack of connection is perhaps not surprising when those involved with generating products and communications at Barclays have long left their own student days behind them. Without sufficient empathy it's all too easy to slip into either a patronizing tone or a faux-cool jargon. Barclays saw that the tone of the offer had to be 'for students by students' and to reinforce that they created a student-to-student platform called **www.100voices.co.uk**, where 100 students shared their experiences with others. For the marketing team, the student input provided the tonal position, the elements of the proposition and the hierarchy of those elements. The resulting communication was radically different from previous Barclays' advertising. For Barclays this was also an experiment, but one they felt confident enough to implement without further research. And as it seems to have been successful in generating new accounts and improving market share as well as winning a prestigious UK Money facts award in 2011, Barclays plan to use co-creation methods in future.

The enthusiasts

A particular challenge facing many organizations, especially those in volatile industries, is the need not just for occasional bursts of creativity, but ongoing, continuous innovation. This creates three requirements. First, organizations that are committed to innovation cannot see it as a satellite operation where researchers, engineers and designers beaver away in splendid isolation but rather they have to view it as something that must be ingrained into the fabric of the organization. It must become part of the culture. Second, knowledge and competencies move around the organization. There are good ideas everywhere that can be tapped into, co-opted and joint-ventured. It does not make sense to try to invent new technologies if there is already good material to work with, that can be adapted. Third, knowing which ideas to funnel through to realization is an inexact process but becomes more precise when consumers and other stakeholders have an active say in product development. These requirements suggest a need for openness and receptivity; a willingness to stretch out beyond the boundaries of the organization; to embrace diversity and the opportunity to create together with others. It is the need to revitalize business models, to find new streams of revenue and to adapt to ever-changing circumstances, that pushes business towards utilizing co-creation as a significant source of innovation. This does not suggest that co-creation is the only source of ideas, but it does imply that 'enthusiasts' see the process as more than just an experiment. Rather they would see it as a journey that can yield significant successes but one that is often beset by backward steps as the desire for conformity and rationality jar against the need for disruption and change.

Intuit's commitment to innovation

The US-based software product and services company, Intuit, provides an apt example of both the opportunities and challenges. Intuit, founded in 1983, provides software programs for small and medium-sized businesses, consumers, healthcare providers and tax professionals. It is a Fortune 1000 company with, in 2010, nearly 8,000 employees and $3.5 billion in revenues. In spite of its impressive track record over its first 20 years of operations, the company found that growth began to plateau. So in 2005 the company embarked on a process designed to stimulate new revenues. While recognizing the need to engage customers and other stakeholders in the process, the priority was to generate a self-sustaining innovation culture. This was partly about building awareness of the importance of innovation among managers and employees and partly about creating an innovation system that could become part of everyday business life. In the initial phase interviews were conducted with managers and potential partners were identified. A long list of groups that could help develop ideas was cut down to four – start ups, suppliers, universities and crowd sourcing. To connect with these groups and begin the process of co-creation, the company organized a number of events.

One example is the Intuit entrepreneur day, where the company invites venture capitalists, start-ups and small companies to submit proposals for collaboration with Intuit. The proposals are then given to the relevant people in the company's business units and they select the ones they would like to progress. The goal here is to generate a short list of between 40 and 60 companies who are then invited to the entrepreneur day where they can 'speed date' with Intuit managers and discuss their ideas. Intuit promises to give a yes or no answer within 48 hours. The benefit to Intuit here is the speed that new revenue opportunities are opened up and new competencies are connected to the business. Intuit define this sort of event as undirected open innovation, but they are also moving to directed innovation whereby the company defines territories and directions it is interested in and then posts them on a site called **www.intuitcollaboratory.com**. This site invites solutions from external parties, who then jointly develop and deliver the concept. This opening up of the organization to stakeholders is energizing but also meets with some resistance, not least because internally there is a perceived threat from the expertise of outsiders, and the innovation arena itself, while fun, can be a distraction from the rational day-to-day requirement to meet business targets.

Alongside the events-based activities has been the development of a system, comprised of five elements. The first is the use of unstructured time – which is also used by 3M and Google. At Intuit, the people who work in product development can use 10 per cent of the working time to develop ideas of their own choosing. Second, every business unit organizes idea jams. This brings people together to brainstorm ideas and develop concepts. To signal the importance of innovation to the organization either the CEO or senior managers attend and take part. Third is the development of an online tool called 'brainstorm' (**www.intuitbrainstorm.com**) which is a cross between a social networking tool and an innovation management tool. The purpose of 'brainstorm' is both to democratize innovation so that everyone can contribute to it and to connect diverse parts of the organization that might rarely come into contact with each other but in combination may have the potential to realize a new business idea. The tool not only allows for people to post ideas but to form groups and to comment on the ideas of others. The fourth element is a prototyping process whereby customers experience, extend and comment on the ideas in development and the fifth is marketplace experiments. The comment could be made that the degree of customer participation is limited here for a company that professes to embrace customer-driven innovation. Yet Jan Bosch, Vice-President of Engineering Process, stresses you don't get to the desired end point immediately. You have to work towards creating a culture that embraces co-creation: 'The intent is to move, as much as possible, to a model where customers are involved from the beginning in determining what is most important in a problem space and in helping to develop a particular solution.'

The question we can pose here is how successful has the Intuit model been? Intuit has had a long record of building communities of users around its various products, who comment on and improve them. Since the mid-2000s there has been a more explicit approach to building connectivity externally and fostering an innovation culture internally. Many of the ideas that have been developed through the new system are typically adjacencies – ideas that have a link to existing products, but new business areas such as health care have also emerged that are making significant contributions to revenue. The company also explicitly set as a goal that it wanted to be seen as an innovation brand and there have been significant shifts on this measure. Bosch argues that it is the totality of the system that makes it effective – that you couldn't have 10 per cent time or the brainstorming tool without the other elements. Together the elements combine to generate a culture which is more willing to take risks: 'The external successes come from the willingness internally to try out new things and to try them out with others. . . we are in the process of teaching the organization to do that.' The target is to increase the 'permeability of the interface between the organization and the outside world.'[11]

Conclusion

Organizations adopt different perspectives to innovation and to the idea of co-creation. These reflect different attitudes to the pursuit of customer connectivity and the cultural milieu of the organizations. Intuit has been pursuing an embedded approach to co-creativity by working with different partners that extend its intellectual capital and by involving customers in the development of products and services. It is still an incomplete project but the intent to be an innovation leader is evident. Barclays sees the approach as an effective alternative to other research methodologies, partly because it carries with it the power of persuasion, but also because it is more vital. In time they may become enthusiasts but the long tradition of rational analysis may place limits on the potential for co-creation. Finally, Apple and Electrolux both stress the value of customer orientation but stop short of co-creation. For them the ethos of product and design expertise inside the organization is very strong. It remains early days for co-creation and it is not yet clear how its role will develop. For the time being we will leave these discussions about the thinking behind co-creation and begin to look at the practicalities of doing it.

Notes

1 Chomsky, Noam and Foucault, Michel, (2006) *The Chomsky-Foucault Debate on Human Nature*. New York: The New Press p 37

2 Pierre D'Huy draws on this distinction in his comparison of the parallel lives of the innovator, Thomas Edison and the inventor, Nikola Tesla. He writes, 'Viewed from the vantage point of today's world it might be said that Edison embodied the method and mindset of the west: pragmatic, results-driven, interested in the market-place, focused on the economics of discovery. Tesla can be seen as more a man of the east: mystical, possessed of a sense of awe with the magnitude of the universe, seeking to deploy science for the greater good of all mankind, focused on the elevation of the spirit, preoccupied with the divine.' 'ET or TE?' *Journal of the Medinge Group*. Published 31 October 2010. Translation: Stanley Moss.

3 The economist, Joseph Schumpeter made this distinction in his 1939 book, *Business Cycles*, where he argued, 'The making of the invention and the carrying out of the corresponding innovation are, economically and sociologically, two entirely different things.'

4 Chesbrough, Henry (2006) *Open Innovation: The New Imperative for Creating and Profiting from Technology*. Boston, Mass: Harvard Business School Press pp 16–17

5 Customer obsession is one of the three core values of the company

6 Leander, Kahney (2009) *Inside Steve's Brain*. London: Penguin Books

7 Krantz, Michael (1999) 'Steve Jobs at 44' *Time Magazine*, October 10

8 Bødker, Susanne and Grønbæk, Kaj (1990) Cooperative Prototyping: Users and Designers in Mutual Activity. Draft paper submitted for *International Journal of Man-Machine Studies*, special issue on CSCW

9 Grønbæk, Kaj, Kyng, Morten and Mogensen, Preben (1997) 'Toward a Cooperative Experimental System Development Approach' in M Kyng & L Mathiassen. *Computers and Design in Context*. Cambridge, Mass: The MIT Press pp 201–38

10 Muniz Jr, A M and O'Guinn, T C (2001) 'Brand Community' *Journal of Consumer Research* 27 (4) pp 412-32

11 Bosch, Jan and Bosch-Sijtsema, Petra M (2011) *Introducing Open Innovation at Intuit* (in *A Guide to Open Innovation and Crowd sourcing: Advice from leading experts in the field,* (2011) edited by Paul Sloane, pp 112–20, London: Kogan Page). London: Kogan Page

PART TWO
Doing it

In the first three chapters the focus has been on the way we think about co-creation. In this second section we will look at how organizations actually practise co-creation with stakeholders such as consumers, employees, citizens and business partners. Here we will look at the cultural environment that facilitates participation as well as the tools that are in use. In particular we will feature content derived from cases and from a community that was set up to help co-create this book. Writers have adopted this approach before, but often the contributors are experts, or what von Hippel calls 'lead users'. These individuals help to provide diversity and perhaps authority, but they do not give direct insight into the feelings and behaviour of consumers towards co-creation. To involve experts only stems from the idea that creativity is the preserve of an elite. One of the fundamental premises of *Brand Together*, however, is that everyone has the ability to be creative in an environment that feels safe and where they feel sufficiently confident to express themselves. Indeed, the willingness and capacity for cooperation necessitates individuals to feel confident. As we will see in the following chapters, one of the key requisites of co-creation is taking the time, especially at the beginning of the process, to establish a bond of trust, both between the organization and the participants and amongst participants themselves.

The Brand Together community, which ran during May and June 2011, involved 236 consumers who had taken part in co-creation activities for different organizations such as Tata, Danone, Sony Music and *The Times*, in the form of online or face-to-face events. The purpose of the community was to create an online forum where people could express their feelings safely on what it was like to be involved in a co-creation process, why they had agreed to participate and what they liked and didn't like. The community also featured discussions on changing perceptions towards the brand they were working with and how they thought co-creation ought to be developed in the future. The point here was both to gain insight into the experience of involvement and to encourage people to help co-create co-creation. The community itself was constructed and moderated. This is clearly different from naturally occurring brand communities where enthusiasts come together to share experiences and discuss ideas based around

FIGURE P2.1   The activities of the Brand Together community (May–June 2011)

Pre-Launched	Week 1	Week 2	Week 3	Week 4
		Ca. 300 consumers from current communities/Big Talks (mix)		
Set-up	**1.** Status Quo: feedback on communities	**2.** You & the brand	**3.** Benchmarking: comparison with other tools	**4.** Looking ahead
	Warm-up	Were you surprised to be contacted to take part? And were your expectations met?	How does the community experience compare with other forms of consumer engagement/interaction?	What would ideal consumer engagement look like?
	Ask for feedback on the online co-creation experience (moderation, tone of voice, impact, activities, interaction, when/where):	Have your perceptions of the brand that has invited you changed since you have been part of the community?	Examples may include: - customer service, CRM - DM, advertising - trad market research (group, surveys)	How should the relationship between brands and consumers develop in the future?
	- likes - dislikes - improvements	Has your relationship (or even your behaviour) with regards to the brand changed at all? If yes, in what ways?	Plot KPI such as level of engagement, creativity, impact, joy	What is the future of (online) co-creation? What would the ideal solution look like? What would you like to see more of?
	What surprised you?	Would you take part again?	What are the benefits and drawbacks of online co-creation?	
	Why did you agree to participate?			
		Outputs		
	Understanding what works with communities and what is broken	Impact of communities on brand loyalty/closeness	Benchmark communities against other tools, understand enefits/drawbacks	Understand where communities should evolve/permission to stretch

a common interest. In these communities rules and structures emerge in response to initiatives and events. With a constructed community the organizers impose certain boundaries, for example the community has a clear life span with an end point, it has a pre-determined direction and use of output, yet the flow of conversation is not rigidly constrained. Within the structure of the Brand Together community and our need for insight in specific areas, there was latitude to allow for the emergence of previously unthought of ideas and themes suggested by the participants. Accordingly there were 21 official project activities plus an additional 146 participant-created activities.

To help structure this section of the book, we will use the model introduced earlier as Figure P2.1.

The model does of course integrate all the various elements, but here we will break it down into its component parts. In Chapter 4, we will take an overall view of the model, setting out the principles that determine an effective approach to co-creation. In the subsequent chapters we will focus on the set up inside the organization, involving individuals, the activities where the brand is co-created and resulting outputs. We will concentrate on consumers as co-creators, but as Hatch and Schultz (2010) remind us, 'brand meaning and value(s)' is the result of engaging with other stakeholders as well. So in Chapter 8 we will look at the other partners. Throughout this section the concept of the brand will be manifest and dominant. We will show how the brand should be seen as a departure point for innovation and the template against which outputs are judged. Undoubtedly the ideology of the brand can be seen as a limit to creativity in that it colours the way both facilitators and participants think and create. It encourages people to notice some things, lend weight to certain perspectives and reject others. It can be a spur to creativity in that it can create connections that would not be seen through a different lens but it can also be a restraint.

Working together

04

- A focus on people
  - Big Chef takes on Little Chef
- Taking time to build trust
  - Four ingredients that help establish trust
- Learning together
- Building concensus for change
- Conclusion

'I can't think of any areas where there is a need for creativity where it can work without a high level of trust.' **LARS NITTVE, FORMER DIRECTOR OF THE MUSEUM OF MODERN ART, STOCKHOLM**[1]

It would be easy to jump straight into the techniques that can be used in co-creation but their effectiveness is determined by the way in which they are used. Therefore in this chapter we will look at the principles that underpin the management of co-creation. Without such principles the danger is that co-creation will become an experiment that does not realize its potential. As the central goal of co-creation is to become closer to customers and other stakeholders, we have to ensure that those managing the process of co-creation work to create cultures that welcome and embrace the ideas of others. This can be a challenge in organizational life. Often employees are encouraged to identify and internalize a set of values that reinforces the idea that they are different from the world outside and from other competitive organizations. Indeed organizations of all types are based on the principle of exclusion – the specific articulation of what they are and, importantly, what they are not. Think Real Madrid v FC Barcelona or Facebook v Google. This sense of otherness is highly valued because it reinforces self-esteem and helps to glue the organization together. It is also prevalent inside organizations where different teams and functions create sub-cultures based on a shared perspective. Yet the downside of this identification process is that if we find it difficult to get close to others we are likely to find it problematic to co-create new products and services. When we emphasize the differences between us inside the organization and the consumers, business partners and entrepreneurs that we may want to connect with, we diminish the ability to empathize. As David Hume argued in 'A Treatise of Human Nature' (1739), we need to have sympathy for others if we want to extend ourselves into relationships and connect with people of similar 'tempers and dispositions'.[2] In other words, employees need to become linked to stakeholders in a relationship based on equality, rather than succumbing to the temptation to stress difference, or worse, superiority.

In this chapter we will look at four key principles that can help to create 'sympathy for others'. In the chapters that follow we will look in more detail at how these principles apply. They are relevant to all forms of collective activity, whatever the techniques employed, because they are fundamental to the way people think and behave. The principles are:

- Focus on people.

  Individuals are willing to take part in co-creation and give of their time because the process is fulfilling. It is an opportunity to socialize with others, to build self-esteem, to learn and to feel one is contributing to something worthwhile.

- Build trust.

  People are willing to share their views and ideas when they trust those around them. Yet trust doesn't just happen. It takes time to build through honesty, openness and transparency.

- Learn together.

  Innovation does not normally appear fully-formed. Usually it is the development of a combination of a big idea and then lots of small evolutionary ideas. The implication is that innovation is iterative and involves a willingness to experiment.

- Build consensus for change.

  Inside the organization the willingness to change is dependent on a number of factors, but one of the keys is involvement. The higher the level of participation, the greater the likelihood of generating real and lasting change.

A focus on people

The disconnect between people inside the organization and those outside has come about with the growing scale of business which removes many people from direct contact with customers and other stakeholders. Senior managers in particular suffer from this isolation because as they become more strategic in their orientation they do not have the time, or perhaps inclination, to engage with customers on a regular basis. Even employees who have regular contact with customers do not necessarily engage in balanced relationships. The American sociologist, Arlie Hochschild observed in *The Managed Heart* (1983) that in service jobs people must detach themselves from their own feelings and 'emotional labour', so that they can act out a defined role that involves the pretence of empathizing with others. The important word here for Hochschild is 'emotional', for she argues it is in the investment in a false self that the individual becomes alienated. When we start to think about innovation, therefore, the task we should set ourselves is to think how we can genuinely connect our real selves with others.

If we accept the value of getting close to customers and partners, we can do so on the basis of two perspectives. One is to see stakeholders as an object; a source of insight to enable innovation and marketing. This is akin to the social systems theorist, Niklas Luhmann, and his approach which sees the organization as an autopoietic system[3] in which 'every trace of the subject' is wiped out.[4] This line of thought does not exclude the individual, but it is the organization itself as an entity that is important. Here we might use different methods to attain insight, including research and co-creation techniques, but the essential attitude is instrumental. We see numbers and segments to be targeted. It is an approach that stresses the difference between insiders and outsiders and tends to dehumanize relationships because the focus is on what the organization can get from customers. The virtue of this perspective is its seeming efficiency in that the organization achieves what it needs from conducting a process and moves on. The problem with the approach, while comfortable for managers preoccupied with strategy, is that it stimulates ways of thinking that ignore human needs for confidence, trust-building and connectivity. That might not seem important if we see branding as a one-way process, but if we believe in the importance of long-term interaction, instrumental thinking tends to show through in the way we behave and communicate.

The alternative human-centric perspective sees stakeholders as connected; as partners in the innovation process. This perspective is based on a principle of reciprocity. The organization treats its stakeholders as insiders who help develop and enhance the brand, while in turn stakeholders feel they have the ability to learn and to influence what their brand may become. Here people within the organization and stakeholders are equals united in a common cause. In this view difference is valued, for it recognizes the individuality of those who participate and the diversity of thought that they bring. We might judge that this perspective perhaps lacks the efficiency of the instrumental approach, where insight can be acquired quickly without overt concern for the feelings of customers, but what the relationship approach clearly offers is the opportunity to build trust. This becomes more important the more we ask of customers. If we are only interested in opinions, then the instrumental approach might be valid, but if we are looking for creativity and engagement then we need people to feel the importance of their involvement and the value of their contribution. As George Orwell noted in an essay on Charles Dickens, 'we can only create if we can care.'[5]

Big Chef takes on Little Chef

In describing these two different perspectives in such a way, it would seem obvious that in the field of co-creation the connected perspective is more appropriate. The difference between the two perspectives can be illustrated through an example.[6] In 2009, Britain's Channel 4 aired a television series called *Big Chef Takes on Little Chef*. The Big Chef was Heston Blumenthal, who has been called the Master of Molecular Gastronomy. His restaurant The Fat Duck, which opened in a small English town in 1995, has three Michelin stars and has been voted the Best Restaurant in the world by an academy of over 600 international food critics, journalists and chefs. Blumenthal is someone who is constantly pushing the boundaries of what is possible: 'We embrace innovation – new ingredients, techniques, appliances, information, and ideas – whenever it can make a real contribution to our cooking.' Little Chef, modelled on US diners, is a chain of 162 roadside eateries established in 1958. It serves fast, basic food. At its height Little Chef had more than 450 restaurants, but it has been in slow decline for many years and has had a succession of not always attentive owners.

The idea of the television series was for Blumenthal to revitalize the Little Chef chain; to create some 'blue sky' ideas. The programmes show this is what Blumenthal is good at. He shuts himself away and experiments with new and adventurous dishes such as Lamb Thyroid Hot Pot with Oysters, and Lapsang Souchong tea smoked salmon. In reality this is far removed from the eggs, bacon and burgers that is the popular and standard fare in Little Chef. It also becomes clear that neither he nor his team have any idea of the brand, the capabilities of the Little Chef staff or the needs of customers. Blumenthal's normal work is within a very specific and rarefied niche. He often protests in the film that he is just an ordinary person but he has no empathy with Little Chef staff, whom he patronizes, nor with the customers whose much-loved Olympic Breakfast is replaced by 'the not-so-full English breakfast' of Parsnip Cereal, Nitro-Scrambled Egg and Bacon Ice Cream with Hot & Iced Tea. Not surprisingly, Blumenthal's ideas are too hard for the cooks to make and rejected by diners. Although he observes what people in Little Chef eat he objectifies them and assumes his expertise will prevail. What makes for entertaining television, of course, is that his lack of empathy generates conflict.

After his initial failure, Blumenthal recognizes the need for a change of tack. Instead of laughing at the Little Chef cooks and their failings, though he rejects the idea they are cooks, saying, 'I can't try and find a cook within Little Chef. They're not cooks, they're not trained chefs', he begins to work with them and involves one of them as a member of his team. He also starts to connect with customers, conducting interviews and asking them what they eat and what they like. He also sets up a breakfast stall at a sporting event and tries to cook good but everyday food. He learns to empathize more and to generate new ideas together with others. His relationship with the Little Chef management is still one of conflict but he begins to establish trust and a more relevant focused creativity that aligns with, but also extends, the idea of the Little Chef brand. One of the interesting aspects of the series is that it provides a narrative over a four-week period of a shift from a perspective based on objectifying customers to one based on engagement and involvement. It signals that it is easy to assume one's expertise will provide the right answer and it reminds us that we have to take time to establish trust if we want to be innovative.

Taking time to build trust

As Blumenthal discovered in *Big Chef Takes on Little Chef* 'we commonly assume others think, want and feel what we ourselves think, want and feel.'[7] This can sometimes be highly valuable for entrepreneurs when their empathies do achieve an intuitive connection, but the assumption of like-mindedness can also be a dangerous one, for it tends to close down our vision of possible alternatives and reduce the potential for creative thinking. It can lead us into thinking that we know more than we do. Thus we need to test and challenge our assumptions[8] – something we should try to achieve with those who actually use our products and services. To do this we need to take the time to establish a safe environment in which to create. We cannot simply ask people to be creative and expect an instant response. Most of the time people are encouraged to conform to societal and organizational norms and to repress their creative tendencies. They might occasionally be asked to take part in a team-building exercise at work or in an amateur dramatic performance or on an online brainstorming session, but for the rest of the time rationality is expected. This makes it hard to achieve the imaginative leaps that fuel novel ideas. Mikhail Bakhtin in *Rabelais and his World* (1984) notes that official events tend to emphasize hierarchy and it is only when this is suspended during carnival that a special type of participation is possible, where people can be 'frank and free' and are liberated from the 'norms of etiquette and decency' imposed at other times.[9] We might argue that co-creation requires this carnival atmosphere to establish a world where people can explore, challenge and laugh together.

When we are in a carnival atmosphere we see things differently. We generate new meanings and we begin to conceive of a future based on our imagination. This can be exciting but it can also create a sense of anxiety as we begin to realize the dangers associated with the new and the uncertain. We move from imagination to an attempt to define and to categorize. In particular, we use language to describe something and give it some communicable shape. When there is imprecision we ask, 'what do you mean by that?' leading to more words that attempt to reduce uncertainty. Weick (2006) suggests that once people start to name the things they see their cognitive processing becomes schema driven rather than stimulus driven which leads to greater intellectual and emotional distance from 'the details picked up by direct perception'.[10]

Some people, such as innovators, are more comfortable with and seem to like uncertainty.[11] They are less concerned by what others think and are better able to escape the frames of the past. They are happy to re-think problems, to come up with the un-obvious and to adopt novel solutions. This is also something that children are better equipped to do. Less constrained by the norms of acceptability and of language and infused with the urge to express themselves, children are better able to just do things. When most adults are asked to draw a picture they start to think about the subject, they become concerned over the meaning of what they will produce, they worry about their ability to execute what they imagine and then they are embarrassed about the result. When children are asked to draw, they leap in and create an image unconstrained by these typical adult fears.[12] The artist, John Baldessari, notes that this fear of the judgement of others begins to emerge when they are about 13 or 14: 'The girls start drawing pretty women and horses. The boys are all tanks and machine guns. All the clichés. But before that they are fantastic. They don't think about art as art at all.'[13]

To create trust in the co-creation process, time needs to be allowed for people to learn to trust each other and the organization. Figure 4.1 shows how this cycle of trust helps to facilitate belief in one's own abilities and those of others and how fear and anxiety is diminished. The longer the cycle runs the deeper the roots of trust. As observed earlier this can slow the initial phase but it delivers depth, and once trust is established a community or group can become very quick in its ability to contribute to a task. In some sense a collective of people builds their own feeling of trust amongst each other, but those involved with establishing and moderating can have a powerful influence on the potential for trust. Four ingredients are important here which we will outline and then develop in the subsequent chapters:

- setting clear boundaries
- setting an example
- providing support
- allowing people to realize their own needs and potential

Four ingredients that help establish trust

When co-creation is initiated by the organization it needs to have **clearly determined boundaries**. This is important for the organization because innovation should be purposive. If co-creation is run to produce new business ideas for Virgin Media, Orange or Barclays, then the outputs need to

FIGURE 4.1   How trust encourages creative behaviour

SOURCE Ind and Watt, 2004

have focus. This is also important for participants, because boundaryless exercises only add to uncertainty and anxiety. We need to have clarity over what is expected of us if we are to contribute creatively. Yet while creative boundaries are important, the facilitation should not be overly prescriptive, especially in early-stage ideation phases. There should be allowance for the community or group to explore unexpected directions and to follow flights of the imagination. The rationale here is simple. We may assume the organization has posed the right question or made the right assumption at the outset but that may not be the case. Every organization is the victim of its own beliefs and sees the world from its own biased perspective, so it's useful to know if the firm-centric view is mirrored by the consumer one. Of course, the challenge here for facilitators is to make the correct judgement on when to allow conversations to digress and when to bring them back to the core.

In research processes, consumers may be asked to answer some questions or deliver an opinion, but they are rarely required to do something explicitly creative. As co-creation seeks to encourage a deeper level of engagement it exposes people to anxiety about social acceptance: Am I doing the right thing? Is what I am doing relevant? Can I express myself effectively? The facilitator can reduce anxiety both by encouraging a positive climate and by **setting an example**. The facilitator enjoys an elevated position within a group or community; a seeming expert who to some degree frames the conversation. If the 'expert' is willing to expose his or her fallibilities by being the first to perform a task, draw a picture or act out a role it reduces the distance. We are also more likely to trust individuals who are transparent in their dealings with us.

When one thinks one knows the answer to a problem, or indeed what the problem is, there is a temptation to control, but the co-creation process should be more open than that. Rather than steering firmly and perhaps interfering with the way a group or community is working, the facilitator

Personal comments made by online community participants

'On top of this, I broke up with my boyfriend of 5 years, a month ago. I know (deep, deep down) that it was for the best and I feel really good about myself and am building up my confidence again, but there is that nagging feeling in the back of my mind saying – what if I never find anyone else?'

'Outside of this community I feel like I have to put on a brave face pretending nothing gets to me, and it is just all backed up in my head affecting how I feel about everything.'

'I've never taken my son swimming – I've told him it is because 'mummy doesn't know how.' The truth is I am plagued by bloating and can't bear the thought of being in a swim-suit.'

needs to have sufficient confidence in the individuals involved to let them explore for themselves. As an example of this, when the Danone-owned yoghurt brand, Activia, which is aimed primarily at women with digestive problems, started a community, it included a 'learn more' link. This was designed to provide participants with deeper insight into the research and insight process they were involved with. Clicking on the link – a very popular feature – explained the theory behind each activity. Such mechanisms as this send a signal about the attitude of the company but we should also note that this self-discovery process does not mean a hands-off approach. There will be occasions when levels of uncertainty rise and people want input and direction. The requirement here is to **provide support** when it is appropriate or necessary. Consequently the facilitation needs to be attentive and empathetic, nurturing the creativity of the people involved and boosting confidence in their abilities.

Finally, when a safe space is established then individuals are willing to reveal more about themselves and to take more risks in developing ideas. In daily life and in working environments there are often constraints that inhibit expression, but a self-contained community or group creates permission for **people to realize their own needs and potential**. Partly this comes about because as participants we get the chance to play out specific roles. In the context of a Dragons' Den group we might have the chance to play out the role of an entrepreneur, or in a drawing exercise we have the chance to express ourselves creatively. We get the chance to do things that maybe we have never done or have not done since childhood. Partly it comes about because we feel we are becoming part of an organization – albeit for a short while – and we have the opportunity to contribute our social and intellectual abilities to create something innovative and valuable for other people. We are engaged in creating a brand together, in defining a space where the possibilities are wide-open. As a consequence, participants start to reveal their whole selves, sometimes talking about things in a community of like-minded individuals that they would not normally discuss with friends and family (see box for example). For a brand owner this depth is vital when considering how to position a product in people's lives and connect with the way a product or service might be used. Cecile Lux of Danone argues that with Activia the traditional use of focus groups to generate consumer insight has some challenges: 'Sometimes it is difficult to go into depth or really speak about intimate subjects. Also when we do focus groups we work with six or seven, but only once. And we really wanted to build something over time because we realized that we needed to develop a relationship to allow people to speak about their intimate problems.'

Learning together

In many innovation processes the typical model is linear. Ideas are developed, filtered, developed and implemented. There may be some toing and froing but there is a progression from early stage development of a number of concepts to the filtering out of ideas that fail to meet the requirements of the brand, resources, finance or likely customer acceptance. In the latter stages a selected idea will be refined and adapted so that it is viable and doable. At the front end of the process there may be some more open-ended research undertaken to gain a better understanding of customer lifestyles. In between the various stages there will be some testing among consumers to check that what is designed actually meets customer expectation. In this process it tends to be the case that different consumers are engaged at different points, so that the people who talk about their lifestyles at the beginning are not the same people who validate the developed product or the marketing campaign.

The linear model has some clear virtues in that it is structured, rational and controllable. Managers inside the organization can still act as experts as they develop an idea and test it at different stages. Yet, as with many models, it has flaws. Since it is a discontinuous process, things can get lost in the gaps: an idea is developed and tested among consumers; information is fed back and then engineers, designers and marketers absorb and refine the idea over a period of time. Meetings are held, some features are discarded and some forgotten, compromises are made and new assumptions emerge. The decisions in the process may be entirely rational or more likely a result of political compromise or messy choices where, as Lindblom observed (1959) everyone has just muddled through and no one can quite remember how they have ended up where they have. At some point of course, it makes sense to go back and research the idea with a new set of potential consumers but a lot of things have now been decided along the way without any consumer input. Also, a linear process is designed around closing down options. If we refer back to Weick's comments about

Frank Gehry and the need to stay open – to act our way into deeper understanding – we should be concerned about a process which is often based on thinking one's way into reducing choices to a viable number.

In contrast, the co-creative model can be iterative, continuous and more organic, inviting input throughout as everyone participates in a co-learning process. The value of this is that individual and collective insight grows. This helps to inspire participants to higher levels of creativity and to provide ongoing input into the development of ideas and prototypes. Rick Jenner, Head of Proposition Development (Home-Mobile) at Virgin Media, observes of its long-running community that it provides a resource for immediate feedback on both strategic and tactical issues; new product decision making as well as competitive insight. It facilitates customer input on detailed concerns where it would be too time consuming to set up a specific piece of research but where some guidance is valuable. This fluidity in co-creation both allows adaption as circumstances change and the possibility to revisit earlier decisions. Rather than sitting ensconced in a meeting room discussing possibilities, users can judge ideas and prototypes.

This willingness to learn can also be extended into the market. This approach has long been practised within the Open Source Movement, where brands such as Apache, Firefox, Thunderbird and Linux have invited users to be participants in a bazaar of co-development. Similarly, the Dutch financial services company, Rabobank has started to experiment with an open source approach to banking products. Using a social network, known as Hyves, the company first set up an open innovation challenge. One of the product concepts that was generated was an account share idea aimed primarily at young people that would enable them to pool money for events. Rabobank then decided to launch a beta version and let customers mould the idea. Innovation Manager, Maarten Korz, says, 'this was a new way of working for us. We put out a product and asked people to help us develop and co-create it. The result was we got a lot of new ideas and the community of customers were very involved and very proud to help us.' Korz argues that if a company is willing to trust people and to share its ideas customers will reciprocate, enabling both sides to learn together.

While the looseness of the co-creation model is valuable in generating and developing new ideas, it does in turn present a set of challenges which need to be managed. First, given the continuity of a co-creation model, the volume of content is significant so resources need to be put in place to filter and mediate the outputs. The raw information is interesting and insightful, particularly when it comes to creating a picture of how a group of people think, but it is not usable as such. We need therefore to filter content by judging its relevance to the task and by looking for the patterns that allow for compression. This requires the mediator of the content to be able to ignore the noise that surrounds material and to use his or her experience to generalize. Second, while co-creation values the developing expertise of participants, there is also the possibility that over time they start to acquire a form of group think and start to act too much like experts. In this case they cease to be representative of typical consumer audiences. Facilitators need to be aware of these possibilities and to keep refreshing the group as it develops.

Build consensus for change

One of the quirks of our research-obsessed age is that leaders often seem to lack the relevant information to make decisions. We can suggest several reasons for this. One is that the glut of information from research, blogs, brand communities, customer feedback process and social media is simply overwhelming. A second is that prejudices bias the understanding of research so that it reinforces already existing ideas about the world. A third is that leaders don't really engage with research. Ask a senior decision-maker to take part in a discussion group or be actively involved in formulating research processes and there is a trudging of feet. The result of this lack of involvement is that research often has to be presented upwards in the organization in an attempt to persuade others. This presents a particular difficulty when dealing with innovative ideas that might imply heavy levels of investment and high risk. Without direct experience of likely customer receptivity towards a new product or service, there may be reluctance to support the development process. Take the example of the Volvo Cross Country, a car that was developed out of insightful early-stage research that focused on the lifestyles of potential buyers and was then scuppered when customer clinic research suggested to managers that it was too high risk to put onto the market – a decision that was only reversed after Subaru successfully launched a competitive product into the same space.

At least while it has a degree of novelty, co-creation seems to enjoy the advantage that it creates an interesting method for direct interaction – something that the managers interviewed for this book feel is powerful. It is akin to the benefits described by Chan Kim and Mauborgne in their paper, 'Tipping Point Leadership' (2003), which demonstrate the value of user experience in reaching decisions.[14] People in senior roles, who can become remote from customers and other stakeholders, seem to be excited by the prospect of direct face-to-face or online involvement and consequently are more willing to attend events and take part in communities. It makes it much easier to achieve top management commitment and to smooth the path of product innovation. Yet this very willingness to become involved is not without its dangers. One of the deliberate ploys in co-creation processes is to try to get the negative attitudes people may feel towards a brand out of the way so that one can then focus on positive creativity. This initial process can sometimes generate a torrent of negativity from customers which can be very hard for managers to accept. The temptation is to defend decisions and to explain why things couldn't be done. This temptation has generally to be refrained from. The negative comments have to be taken on the chin if a downward spiral of accusation and counter-accusation is to be avoided. Secondly, when managers take part in an event or a community there is a tendency to jump to conclusions. Something is said or written which seems to show a new opportunity or confirms an existing bias and the hearer switches off to subsequent arguments. This indicates the need both to encourage managers to stay open to ideas and to recognize the value of a mediator who can weigh the patterns of conversation and provide an insight into the meaning behind the words. Lastly, there is the issue of surprise – or lack of it. Co-creation can generate new concepts that have not been conceived of inside the organization, but equally it can produce thoughts which have already been discussed. The latter may be as useful as radical innovation but seems less exciting.

We will address the issues of managing the process of co-creation more fully later, but we should note for now that innovation requires sensitivity to the needs of people in the organization. It certainly seems a positive factor that senior managers are willing to engage with co-creation processes. Yet there is also potential here to be a victim of one's own success. For as co-creation becomes integrated into the organizational fabric, so it places demands on the smooth running of day-to-day business. There are still targets to be met, strategy meetings to attend and schedules to stick to. The disruption that innovation brings may not be welcome. As Jan Bosch says of Intuit's push towards innovation, 'we are in the process of teaching the organization to try out new things with others. My biggest challenge is to drive the internal willingness, absorption capacity and prioritization of collaborative innovation efforts.' This suggests the need for managers to be Janus-like, focused on getting closer to customers while looking inwards to generate the involvement and commitment that will enable co-created ideas to be implemented. Without this there is the real possibility that innovation efforts will be wasted and customer interest in participation diminished through inaction.

Conclusion

This chapter has set out a set of principles that help to ensure the effectiveness of co-creation methods. The principles are rooted in the idea that co-creation often asks a lot of customers and other stakeholders. It asks them to give of themselves and to contribute their intelligence and creativity to help organizations become more successful. Whereas other research methods ask less of people, the significance of the input here moves the connection between the organization and the participant away from the transactional and towards the relational. This creates a set of psychological obligations which must be met if people are to continue giving of themselves. We have suggested here that the key elements involve the adoption of a human-centric (non-instrumental) view of participants, a willingness to take the time at the beginning of the process to build trust, a commitment to openness and transparency, the humility to recognize that the question posed at the outset may not be the right question, the capability to learn through the trial and error of experiment and prototyping and finally the involvement of key decision-makers in the process.

Of course it can be argued that not all these elements need to be in place to have a functioning co-creation method, but the likelihood of successful innovation is heightened if an environment is created in which people can genuinely create together.

Notes

1 Nittve was previously the founding director of Tate Modern in London and director of the Louisiana Museum of Modern Art in Denmark. He is now leading a new cultural and museum project in Hong Kong, called M+.

2 Hume, David (1969) *A Treatise of Human Nature*. First published 1739/1740. London: Penguin

3 Luhmann, Niklas (2003) 'Organization.' *Autopoietic Organization Theory: Drawing on Niklas Luhmann's Social Systems Perspective*. Ed. Tore Bakken and Tor Hernes. Oslo: Abstrakt Forlag, pp 31–52

4 Thyssen, Ole (2003) 'Luhmann and Management: A Critique of the Management Theory in Organisation Und Entscheidung.' *Autopoietic Organization Theory: Drawing on Niklas Luhmann's Social Systems Perspective*. Ed. Tore Bakken and Tor Hernes. Oslo: Abstrakt Forlag, p 222

5 Orwell, George (1981) *A Collection of Essays*. New York: Harvest Books, p 100

6 Watt, Cameron and Ind, Nicholas (2011) 'Big Chef-Little Chef: The Bear-Traps and Pitfalls That Can Hinder Design Thinking.' *Design Principles and Practices* 5.2, pp 33–39

7 Chiles, Todd H, Tuggle, Christopher S, McMullen, Jeffery S, Bierman, Leonard and Greening, Daniel W (2010) 'Dynamic Creation: Extending the Radical Austrian Approach to Entrepreneurship.' *Organization Studies* 31.1, pp 7–46

8 Nietzsche argues that the trick is not really about having the courage of one's convictions, 'rather it is having the courage to attack one's convictions!!!' Nietzsche, Friedrich (1974) *The Gay Science* Trans. Walter Kaufmann from second edition, 1887. New York: Vintage, footnote p 152

9 Bakhtin, Mikhail (1984) *Rabelais and His World*. Trans. Helene Iswolsky. Bloomington, Indiana: Indiana University Press

10 Weick, Karl E (2006) 'The Role of Imagination in the Organizing of Knowledge.' *European Journal of Information Systems* 15, pp 446–52.

11 Ekvall, Göran (1997) 'Organizational Conditions and Levels of Creativity.' *Creative Management and Development (3rd Edition)*. Ed. Jane Henry. London: Sage Publications, pp 135–46

12 The Swiss artist, Paul Klee, recognized this explicitly when in his early twenties he decided to try to unlearn what he knew about the world and art and the goal of making acceptable pictures. Instead he set about trying to paint like a child ('as though newborn'), without the constraints of adulthood.

13 Aspden, Peter (2009) 'Flirting Game'. *Financial Times*, October 3: Life and Arts, p 10

14 Chan Kim, W and Mauborgne, R (2003) 'Tipping Point Leadership.' *Harvard Business Review* 81(4), pp 60–69

The set up

05

- Getting to the right Final Big Question
  - Brand strategy and Jumeirah's FBQ
- Generating organizational traction
- Designing a co-creation programme
  - The different benefits of online and live co-creation
- Conclusion

'*To contemplate is to question.*'[1] GILLES DELEUZE

Having defined the key principles that should underpin any co-creation approach, in this chapter we will start to focus on the practicalities of instituting a process of working together with stakeholders. Of course the temptation is to gloss over this phase on the assumption that the organization already knows enough about itself, its competitive environment and the question it would like to pose. Surely in the process of developing organizational strategy there has been an objective analysis of strengths, weaknesses, opportunities and threats and a definition of the innovation themes? There may certainly have been analysis, but there are several reasons why scepticism might still be valuable. First, as the philosopher, Gilles Deleuze notes, 'most cultures refuse to allow their own senses and values to be questioned – they become a set of incorrigible fictions.' In other words, when we see the world through cultural blinkers, we tend to miss things, especially the weak signals that lie beyond our range of vision. This means that it is easy to ignore competitors who come from outside the normal competitive set, such as when telecoms operators become banks and computer companies become handset providers. Second, strategies are rooted in non-objective ideas about the past and imagination about the future. They reduce the complexity of experience to something that can be articulated and understood. As Mintzberg *et al* remind us, 'it has to be realized that every strategy, like every theory, is a simplification that necessarily distorts reality. Strategies and theories are not reality themselves, only representations (or abstractions) of reality in the minds of people.'[2] Finally, while there is an organizational need for analysis it is in the process of acting that strategies come to life. While we might have determined a direction intellectually, there ought to be a willingness to allow for adaptation as new circumstances emerge and as learning takes place through action.

The sceptical approach should encourage two seemingly contradictory attitudes. On the one hand the organization needs to be rigorous in its analysis of itself and its environment. On the other it needs to be reflective and adaptive. Yet these attitudes are not exclusive. The organization has to use analysis not to close down thought but to open it up; to challenge itself and its assumptions and to explore new possibilities. This should remind us of Marcel Proust's observation that we are perched on a pyramid of past life – an interesting metaphor because it suggests the scale of previous experiences that sit under the perceptions we have of the world. Managers have to try to balance the impact of the past with the sense of the future, not to find answers but to pose the right question. The rigour involved in this early co-creation phase is needed to reach what can be called the Final Big Question (FBQ). A question that is of sufficient weight, relevance and interest that it motivates and excites the organization and the stakeholders who will help to co-create an answer.

Getting to the right Final Big Question

The importance of defining the right Final Big Question should not be underestimated. If the initial analysis leads to a FBQ that is imprecise or irrelevant then the outputs will be questionable. For example, if McDonalds posed the question 'What should our restaurants be like in three years time?' it would lead to a co-creation approach that was focused on the possibilities suggested by this specific time frame and the object of the restaurant itself. The problem with the question is its lack of an explicit focus on the customer experience and a time scale that encourages an extrapolation of the present rather than imagining the future. The question also lacks a sense of the customer segment. By leaving this open we might infer that the restaurant chain is interested in the input of all types of customers and non-customers. Yet that might not be the case. If the goal is to attract existing customers to higher levels of purchase frequency or encourage a group of non-customers to try the experience, then that needs to become part of the FBQ. What we should be seeking therefore in the question is an important human-centric issue that incorporates the following:

- A future oriented, inspiring dilemma that goes beyond the obvious and requires intellectual and creative input.
- A business and brand relevant issue that is strategically important.
- A clear articulation of the stakeholder segment(s) and their attitudes and behaviour.

● A focus on real stakeholder needs; a subject or theme that people can easily understand and they can see will make a real difference to them or the people they care about.

Bearing these attributes in mind the initial phase of diagnostic research should be aimed at creating precision in the FBQ while maintaining an openness to future possibilities. Here the goal is to better understand the current market situtation of the brand relative to competitors and the future trends that may impact on performance, key stakeholder attitudes and behaviour by segment, and the nature of the organizational structure and culture. Much of this information may already exist inside the organization, but it may also require additional analysis, observation and research that may indeed question current beliefs. Here we can incorporate ethnographic studies to better understand customer tribes through direct engagement. This might involve observing families and their rituals or extreme users of a product or how cultural tourists behave in different places. Schouten et al,[3] note, in their ethnographic study of female Harley-Davidson riders, that consumption subcultures offer the benefit of a dual insight. First, in that they are active co-creators with marketers of 'brand meanings, of styles, of product categories and modifications'. Second, in that because the tribe is an artefact of the market, 'subcultures of consumption feel the effects of market forces more so than other subcultures such as those with ethnicity or religion at their foundations.' Also as existing customer segments are both valuable and often adept at new product development, ethnographic studies of the interaction between the brand and the loyal user can be particularly fruitful. However, if the business needs of the brand dictate that new segments should be engaged, then the organization should focus on generating an understanding of the lifestyles of non-users and head in the direction of those blue oceans that can generate above average returns. For example, in the case of Kuoni, the luxury travel and tour operator, the segmentation question was concerned not with existing customers but with new ones – the dilemma in this instance being which new customers? Should it be all people who buy premium holidays, including online, or only those who already buy through a tour operator? The answer to this could only be decided by a deeper understanding of the behaviour of the potential audiences and an assessment of market potential. Kuoni opted for the latter segment.

While this FBQ phase may appear rooted in typical analytic methods such as desk research and interviews, there is also room to unlock thinking with more creative processes. This might involve group based exercises in which people speculate, 'what if we do nothing and the organization just drifts?' What would happen to customers; what might competitors do; what would happen to business performance? The value of this discussion is that it helps people to imagine a future scenario where other players are active and the organization is passive. This reminds everyone of the dangers of inertia and the fluidity of the environment while encouraging managers to focus on the most important issues. Similarly, a group might also discuss

Getting to the right FBQ

> Jumeirah: How can we invent the luxury hospitality experience of the future?
>
> Virgin Media: What does a truly consumer-centric growth strategy look like?
>
> Visa: Why should we care about payment cards?
>
> Kraft: What is the biggest role that Kraft can play in people's lives, all round the world?
>
> Etihad: What is the best experience we can deliver on the A380 given that we are not the first mover in the market?

what the world would be like without the organization or the brand. By using such an extreme situation it is possible to pinpoint which segments are most closely linked to the organization, what their competitive alternatives are and which attributes generate most value.

Brand strategy and Jumeirah's FBQ

To illustrate the context of co-creativity, we can turn to the set-up process of the Dubai-based luxury hotel and leisure company, Jumeirah Group. In 2005, the Group defined a brand essence, based on the idea of 'stay different', that was both a commitment statement to customers and an ongoing challenge to itself. Having articulated the brand the question arose as to the meaning of 'stay different'. The implication was that difference *per se* was not so important but difference that created an emotional connectivity around which a relationship could be built, might be. This need to uncover the meaning of the brand, together with customers, was allied to a business strategy built on aggressive growth and brand extension and evolution. CEO Guy Crawford also stresses that the implementation of the strategy had to be based on 'real feedback from customers' and 'the key attributes that we wanted the brand to deliver'.

The Jumeirah management understood that in spite of having continuous contact with customers there was little actual dialogue. In-room questionnaires and brief chats with customers didn't provide sufficient depth as to what customers really wanted. The FBQ for Jumeirah focused on the future long-term realization of its brand essence in conjunction with existing customers such as business travellers and families. In particular, with so many competitor brands offering luxury experiences, the challenging task for managers and customers together was to find significant and relevant innovations that could convey real difference and encourage repeat visits and positive word-of-mouth recommendations – a factor that is increasingly important in a Trip Advisor mediated world. Echoing the danger of drift, Bill Walshe, then Chief Marketing Officer of Jumeirah, points out, 'I think we were complacent, as a lot of hotel companies were. We believed that there was sufficient interaction with the customer. But we came to realize that market research was after the event and anything it might lead us to was reactive and that what we needed to do was to take that consumer engagement and communication and make it proactive.'

Generating organizational traction

With all intervention processes there is both a need to understand the issues and a need to gain traction inside the organization. In developing the FBQ attention needs to be paid to understanding the needs and perhaps fears of internal stakeholders. This is important for two reasons. First, one of the key success factors in significant co-creation processes is the participation and endorsement of senior managers from sometimes diverse parts of the organization. This is important symbolically for participants from inside and outside the company because senior manager involvement indicates that innovation is significant and that the ideas generated will have the opportunity to be realized. For those involved in co-creation it quickly becomes demotivating to feel that what they do lacks relevance or impact. As Rick Jenner of Virgin Media observes of the challenge of co-creation, 'if you go out and say to people you want to involve them and then you don't act upon it, you begin to lose credibility quite quickly. . . in a community you are asking for people's time and contribution and what they expect in return is for things to be better and you therefore have to be able to prove that what they have said has made a difference.' Second, while it is convenient to talk of the organization as an 'it', as if it was some unified system, the reality is that organizations are riven by competing interests and different needs. Realized innovation does not usually happen simply because the insight or marketing team promotes an idea, nor because the engineering group develops a technical improvement. Rather it requires the coming together of different disciplines to help create a customer relevant idea and then to realize it. When people work in isolation, solutions tend to be partial and beset by internal conflicts.

Steve Johnson relates how Apple use an approach called concurrent or parallel production, whereby 'all the groups – design, manufacturing, engineering, sales – meet continuously through the product development cycle' as they iteratively evolve solutions together. It is a process that creates 'clash and connection' between the different disciplines but aims to keep 'the conversation open to a diverse group of perspectives'.[4] The concurrent approach was also adopted by Volvo in the development of the Cross Country. Until this model, development had been linear. The engineering team would lead off and develop a technically superior product and then it would move through the different departments, eventually arriving with the marketing team who would have to figure out an angle to present to the market – invention not innovation. With the Cross Country, by contrast all the teams were involved from the outset and were inspired by the idea of the brand and the insight into customers' lifestyles. The Concept Manager, Sara Öhrvall, says, 'my insight is that these people (the team assembled to work on the Cross Country) hadn't worked together before. Previously the process was sequential. In this case we worked in a team, which meant the design people and others could explain things. Success has a lot to do with communication. The engineering people, especially, just loved being told about the consumers and how they would use the car and why they would love this or that feature.'[5] Both Volvo and Apple demonstrate the importance of widespread internal engagement that emphasizes customers and other stakeholders rather than internally focused requirements. The principle of openness aims to avoid the damage that internal politics can inflict on a change process, especially if issues go unacknowledged or certain disciplines are excluded from the development process. An implication of this is to try to make the FBQ discussion as inclusive as possible and to ensure that key departments and individuals are involved.

In structuring the co-creation process itself a number of factors need to be taken into account, not least being the commercial value connected to answering the FBQ. If the organization sees co-creation as an experiment perhaps to be conducted on a tangential product or service, then the commercial benefit is likely to be low. This would indicate that the investment in co-creation might be limited to either a short-term online community or a limited number of face-to-face events. On the other hand, if co-creation becomes an integral part of the innovation process, such as at Virgin Media, it might become a key ongoing mechanism for generating insight and creating new products and services. Equally, if the FBQ is very significant for the organization then the need for robust input becomes vital. For example, the role of the National Lottery Commission (NLC) is to protect the interest of lottery participants whilst maximizing proceeds for good causes. This means balancing the needs and views of regulators, journalists, pressure groups, charities and citizens, some of whom can be highly critical. For NLC getting this balance right is fundamental to their success, even their existence. One clear advantage that NLC enjoys is that its subject matter (bringing together gambling and supporting good causes) generates a high level of interest. Both topics are highly emotive, much discussed in the media and there is no shortage of opinions about them. Consequently, participants approach an NLC community with plenty to get off their chests. Such high levels of motivation to express opinions and co-create can also be found in niche areas such as Star Trek tribes, Cliff Richard fan clubs or Apple Newton followers.[6] Equally when the brand itself is seen to be exciting then motivation is not likely to be an issue. For example, people that have participated in a community for *The Times* newspaper and then in the Brand Together community are typically very engaged:

> I would add that this site, and the Times Plus site I migrated from, seem to have intelligent and sensible contributors which makes it a pleasure to discuss things.

The thing that sets this apart, which applied equally to the previous Times group, is that there is a sense that this is more of an eclectic group of people who have something in common and whose views are usually worth reading. I have been a member of other groups in the past but it was too big, it didn't have a community feel. I have a feeling if this group were all invited to a massive function we would quickly find sparkling conversation, wit and banter.

I enjoyed the Times community because it was an opportunity to influence a product I use every day and that I have strong views about. Also I have a general curiosity about the world and the people in it, so enjoy discussing diverse topics in an intelligent debate and seeing the views of others.

Not all organizations are in the fortunate position of *The Times*. Some categories and products elicit lower levels of interest. If this is the case then mechanisms such as competitions and rewards may need to be introduced to engage and excite people. More importantly, transparency becomes paramount. Whatever the category or product people are far more likely to be motivated if they feel the organization is being open with them, sharing knowledge and constraints. There are sometimes valid reasons why companies feel constrained about sharing. Rick Jenner notes that within Virgin Media, 'there is a fear around telling consumers too much', for even though they operate a closed community, there is still the possibility of information leaking to outsiders. Still, Jenner notes that the more you do share the better the engagement – an idea that links with Spinoza who argued that institutions should not succumb to the temptation to 'transact everything behind the backs' of people. Instead they should be confident that individuals will participate in a positive and active way if the facts and issues are fully shared with them.[7]

Indeed the principle of transparency also applies inside the organization, because we should note that those charged with initiating co-creation need to manage the expectations of their colleagues who are likely to be wondering whether something radical that no one has ever imagined before is going to emerge or more likely a re-framing of an existing concept. This of course depends on a large number of factors ranging from the scope of the FBQ, to the amount of time and resource allocated to the process, to the type of people involved, to the support provided. As a generalization, the more the organization is willing to share the greater the likelihood of higher levels of creativity. Sometimes people do come up with previously unthought of ideas but also they often validate existing directions while adding new insights. Also, as we saw in the case of the Barclays Student Account, one of the benefits can be how to combine the elements of a product and present it in the appropriate tone of voice.

Designing a co-creation programme

To design an effective co-creation programme, the organization needs to take into account the preparatory work it has done in defining a FBQ and its level of ambition and resources with regards to innovation. Co-creation can be seen as a project with a fixed start and end point or a way of life that provides ongoing insight and creative input. Whatever the time and scope of the process, boundaries, brand, customer, technology and economics, need to be specified, priorities determined and outputs agreed. While we argue for a willingness to adapt as co-creation processes evolve, we would argue that this is far better done within a framework. In other words, we need both freedom and order for effective creativity.

The key decision that needs to be made at this design stage is the means of co-creation. This is about deciding to use live or online or a combination of the two. While there is a tendency to think of co-creation in terms of online communities, direct face-to-face co-creation has a long history with roots in many areas such as psychology, philosophy and innovation history (see below, Dr Nick Coates on 'The Co-creation mix'). Before the emergence of online communities there was wide recourse to the interaction of a large number of consumers and other stakeholders with company managers in intensive co-creation sessions involving typically between 25 and 80 people. Two of the pioneers of this approach, Roy Langmaid and Mac Andrews described in detail in their paper, 'Theory and Practice in Large Groups', how these co-creation sessions function. They also acknowledged that there were other variants of the idea: 'Since we pioneered this approach back in 1991 we are aware that many of our peers and colleagues have developed their own approach to all kinds of experimental workshops, many involving large groups.'

The different benefits of online and live co-creation

In the online world naturally occurring groups and the emergence of participatory environments such as Wikipedia, YouTube and Facebook have brought the idea of communities to the fore. Consequently people have become used to online discussion and creation and largely understand the protocols of engagement. From a co-creation perspective, while some of the aspects of online and live can be seen as similar, there are clearly differences which make them appropriate to certain contexts and tasks, as shown in the box:

Online	Live
Asynchronous	Real time
Continuous	Time limited
Multi-dialogues	One conversation at a time
Degree of anonymity	Physical
Individual within a collective	Teams
Better for evolution	Better for revolution
Unfolding	Intense

The attributes of each world offer certain specific benefits. For example asynchronous conversations that last over an extended period of time

FIGURE 5.1   Example of a co-creation programme

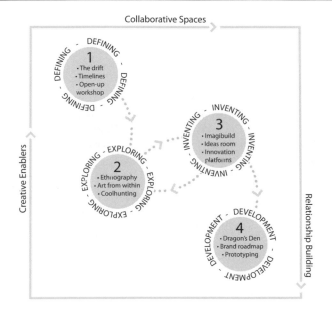

create a different context for the emergence of meaning compared with live. The fact that online conversations are non-linear and allow for revisiting provides the opportunity for reflection and regression. Participants can of course make a more spontaneous comment and move on but they can also go back, question and create new strands in more than one conversational thread at a time. In a live context conversation takes place, a shared meaning emerges from the dialogue and a new stage is reached. People can attempt to revisit previous discussions but they do not have written transcripts with which to determine exactly what was said and so they have to sense the past. Whereas in a community a conversation unfolds as layers are added, in a face-to-face environment there is a greater degree of intensity as we exchange thoughts not only with our voices but also with our bodies. That is part of the reason why sensitive subjects are often best tackled live where there is still a degree of anonymity.

Physical interaction makes a lot more sense when the co-creation process is concerned with three-dimensional situations or service experiences. To create a restaurant experience with McDonalds customers, an airline cabin with Etihad passengers or a hotel environment with Jumeirah guests is difficult online. People need to move through space, interact and play roles to determine their real needs and the viable solutions. Ask an online community to design an airline cabin and the immediacy of interaction with a group of people is missing. By way of contrast evolving a product prototype over several different stages or asking people to review different approaches to brand development is ideally suited to the online world, because these are situations that unfold through evolution. Overall this suggests that the live environment is better suited to the intensity of radical creativity, whereas the online is better adapted for evolutionary creativity. The combination of online and live is ideal when an organization wishes to co-create an innovation and then carry the idea through to implementation; especially important where long lead times are involved in development, as the impact of technological and market changes as they occur can be tested with the community.

Once the co-creation approach is agreed the specific activities within an event or a community can be determined based on the nature of the requirement. Working from the FBQ and the brief, a series of interactions can be planned within the relevant areas. Alongside the activities, attention also needs to be paid as to whom to involve and when. Inside the organization, key people need to be encouraged to participate in the online and live activities and from outside the segment needs to be finally determined and supplemented with any relevant experts. While we adhere strongly to the idea that everyone can be creative, there may also need to be people involved who possess a specific competence. In the case of Etihad, for example, the designers of the cabin interior also took part in the events, both to learn directly from potential customers and to contribute their know-how to the participating groups.

CASE STUDY   Dr Nick Coates describes the
emergence of co-creation

The co-creation mix

Co-creation, first and foremost, starts from a challenge – to the notion of authorship and the authority of the lone creator in particular. And by starting here I'm hoping to emphasize that the culture of co-creation is wider and more diverse than the mainstream interpretation seems to suggest. The idea of 'creation' isn't just about the creation of things, it's about interpretation and meaning-making. Meaning is always co-created. As Roland Barthes argued in his infamous article 'La mort de l'auteur' (1968), power needs to be handed increasingly to users: *'a text's unity lies not in its origin but in its destination... to give writing its future, it is necessary to overthrow the myth: the birth of the reader must be at the cost of the death of the author.'* [8] This is particularly relevant if we want to look at co-creation through the lens of brands and a concept of brand that's all about dialogue not monologue, about readership, not authorship, about ownership by consumers not producers.

Of course in the wider business and marketing community, it's Prahalad & Ramaswamy we have to credit with popularizing the concept of co-creation and bringing the word to prominence. Their 2000 article 'Co-Opting Customer Competence', which appeared in the *Harvard Business Review* in the January of that year, was followed by a book-length study *The Future of Competition*.[9] Their focus was on the creation of 'value' between the customer and the firm rather than solely inside the firm. Moving beyond an obsession with assets held internally by companies, Prahalad & Ramaswamy argue that firms that succeed in the 21st century will do so on the basis of their ability to connect with partners and focus on personalization for customers. Iconic brands that embraced co-creation included Harley Davidson (bikers customizing their vehicles), Nike (with their trainer customization portal Nike ID) and the Apple iPod / iPhone (device as co-creation platform where users add value to the experience by uploading their own content and choosing apps). These examples are reflective of the greater interest in management circles with co-creation at the point of production or in-use and the emphasis on the value chain as the major framework for thinking about co-creation.

But there is another facet to the evolution of co-creation, another way of telling the story. One essential sub-story revolves around design and innovation, in other words customer involvement in the 'fuzzy front end' of the product and service development process. In many fields, including market research, this is the dominant use and meaning of co-creation. People will talk about 'having co-created X or Y' – the focus is on the output, on things. But it's a focus on creating *new* things that are more relevant, quicker to bring to market, and in many cases more innovative than in a traditional expert-driven R&D 'stage-gate' process. While involving customers / users in helping shape products and services is relatively new to market research and certainly new to many companies, there are precedents from the design world that began in the 1970s with a Scandinavian approach called 'participatory design'. Put very simply, the idea of participatory design is that if you want to create usable services, spaces, products you are best off involving the people who are going to have to use them. There is an important lesson in this branch of the co-creation story in that involving future users of services opens up an area of application – public services and spaces – that is often overlooked. Interaction between stakeholders changes the often fraught relationship between producer, deliverer, and user. In our work we have used large-scale co-creation techniques to engage, for example, citizens, insurers, medics and government in conceiving a new healthcare system for Dubai; similarly Charles Leadbeater, author of *We-Think*, has argued that co-creation can help create better public healthcare and education services because 'a new set of relationships between users, workers and professionals lies at its heart'.[10]

The open source movement is one of the real success stories of the late 20th century and a trend that has evolved in parallel with co-creation. The idea that a product like Linux would be running nuclear power stations as well as netbooks on a large scale would have seemed preposterous 50 years ago. Ditto Wikipedia. But beyond its basic utility open source is an idea. It starts with a gift (as in a gift, not money-based, economy). It starts with opening. It starts with an act of humility. And, as Linux shows, the gift given without expectation of immediate return, can generate far more than other models of production. To adapt an old saying, humility is the mother of co-creation. And what happens when we work in this way? Well, Eric Raymond has described the resulting, bottom-up, structure as more like a bazaar (or souk) and less like top-down structures like cathedrals. Cathedrals are highly planned, highly controlled, beautiful in their own way, but less organic. For anyone involved in co-creation, our mental framework, our approach and our expectation, should be structured chaos. The souk has its own order, its own logic, its own patterns… you just have to be willing to get 'lost in the funhouse' from time to time knowing that, to quote

John Barth, at the end of a turning you'll find your babouche-seller. But while open source starts with the same spirit as co-creation, because of the strong technology focus it tends to attract expert co-creators or 'lead users' rather than 'average' users.

A key dimension that has emerged in the co-creation debate – beyond the question of where in the value chain it occurs – relates to belief (or lack of belief) in the creativity of consumers. Many co-creation practitioners have adopted the lead-user, or 1 per cent-er model, working with semi-experts or people screened for their creative skills. We tend to favour a more populist approach based on a view of universal creativity. But we believe equally in the need for the right conditions and process and this is where the psycho-therapy tradition becomes important in painting a picture of the evolution of co-creation. Running co-creation processes needs us to help groups reach new joint insights which can lead to breakthroughs or, equally, old ideas in new and more relevant combinations.

The tradition that includes the likes of Freud, Jung, Winnicott and Kurt Lewin empha-sizes safety and relationship needs, but also ways of expressing unfiltered desires, in par-ticular through what Jung calls 'guided fantasy' and play. The use of techniques such as 'art from within' has its origins in a combination of Winnicott's doodling techniques (which he deployed in his work with children) and French surrealism (automatic writing). The idea of 'serious play' is, I think, an important component of the co-creation palette, but one that actually features quite rarely in a public debate that typically highlights rationality and the inexorable funnelling of the innovation process. Gamification is increasingly in vogue currently as a way of delivering 'serious play', but some of the more experimental and lib-erating techniques explored by creativity and innovation practitioners in the 1980s, not to mention structural processes like Open Space Technology,[11] also need a look-in. Working with live groups to create breakthroughs is an approach that partially starts with Lewin's Action Research and becomes more creative and collaborative in subsequent decades. Technology has broadened its scope and its reach, but it doesn't originate with the birth of the internet.

But there's another thought derived from psychotherapy that stands in opposition to terms that compete for attention with co-creation. Things like crowdsourcing often assume that the answer is 'out there somewhere' and that wide-scale distribution can help us find the answer. In co-creation, the process generates the 'answer' and, in many cases, the answer can only be reached through the process – not by an individual (gen-ius) in isolation stewing over a problem and waiting for the eureka moment. This parallels the process of group psychotherapy and group analysis, in particular where, instead of therapist analysing patient, the group reaches insights and direction through the process of interaction and mutual self-commentary. Similarly, co-creation needs to start from the assumption that while the answer is 'out there', the 'there' is always in the future. The group can get there but only by sharing time, relationships and collaboration.

As with many concepts, the 'arrival' of co-creation has as much to do with parallel developments such as the mainstream adoption of internet technologies, the pioneering work of some companies, the growth of social, collaboration and customization technolo-gies. Some accounts of co-creation read as though the practice sprang to life fully-formed post-Prahalad. And yet, as our timeline shows, co-creation has roots stretching back to the mid 20th century if not before.

In my view it's more helpful to see the current co-creation space as a coming-together of diverse strands of thought that span psychotherapy, management science, innova-tion and open innovation, design, literary theory, creativity practice. From these various

FIGURE 5.2

A timeline of co-creation

Prehistory	Foundations	Emergence	Applications	Formalising	Blossoming
1900 - 50	1950 - 80	1980s	1990s	2000 - 2008	2008 -
Philosophy Nietzsche Psychology Freud Winnicott	Counter Culture 1968 Situationism Barthes *[Death of the Author]* Findhorn Garden (1976)	Creativity & Decision- Making Processes Harrison Owen (1980) OpenSpace3 (1985)	Commercial Programmes British Airways Breakthrough Programme Experience Economy Pine & Gilmore	Agencies Appear Communispace Sense Worldwide (1999) Promise (2003) Face (2005) Value CC Prahalad School Service Dominant Logic	Agency white papers Promise Fronteer Strategy Sense Worldwide CCA founded Books
			Open Source Linux	Social Media Crowdsourcing Jeff Howe	Tech explosion
Organisational Psychology Kurt Lewin			Senge (1990) *The Fifth Discipline*	Cambrian House	Co-creation Forum founded

strands, we can pinpoint some defining ideas that, together, describe what co-creation is all about:

- from **participatory design** – involving end users leads to better products

- from **literary theory** – meaning is co-created, interpretation a two-way process

- from the **open source** movement – starting with a gift produces more generous returns

- from **collaborative innovation** – breakthroughs come from 'group genius' not lone epiphanies

- from **psychotherapy** – the answer or insight isn't already out there waiting, it has to be discovered with others.

Woven together, these strands create a rich texture but increasingly the co-creation space is dominated by technology-driven discourse. More and more co-creation is being stripped down and pulled into the orbit of things like mass customization, which are co-creative in a rather restricted, value-chain-obsessed, way. This is a limiting perspective on a potentially rich discipline. Limiting, because it fails to acknowledge the cultural, theoretical and practical origins of the co-creation idea, an idea which is older than the term itself.

Seen in this way, co-creation is ultimately an approach, an attitude, a mindset and, potentially, a new way of managing brands and businesses.

Dr Nick Coates is Research Director of Promise

Conclusion

This chapter has focused on the practicalities of setting up a co-creation programme. This might make co-creation seem a structured process and in some respects it is, because the organization needs to determine innovations that are strategically relevant and participating stakeholders need to have relevant boundaries to work within. Within this structure, however, there should be an allowance for organic development. In addition to the Final Big Question, which provides the overall focus, there are plenty of opportunities to explore sub-themes and to learn from participants who have a tendency to want to explore areas of interest in addition to the mainstream discussions. Rather than trying to stop this meandering, the organization should encourage it. There are opportunities to learn about people's whole lives and for organizations to be surprised by how customers see their brands. This suggests that managers have to work on becoming participative and being receptive to the co-creation experience.

Notes

1 Deleuze, G (1968) *Difference and Repetition* (Différence et Répétition, Presses Universitaires de France). Trans. P Patton (2004) Continuum, London

2 Mintzberg, H, Ahlstrand, B and Lampel, J (1998) *Strategy Safari.* p 17, FT Prentice Hall, Harlow, Essex

3 Schouten, J, Martin, D and McAlexander, J (2007) 'The Evolution of a Subculture of Consumption', in *Consumer Tribes,* ed. B Cova, R Kozinets and A Shankar, pp 67–75, Butterworth Heinemann, Oxford

4 Johnson, S (2010) *Where Good Ideas Come From: The natural history of innovation,* Allen Lane, London pp 170–71

5 Ind, N and Watt, C (2004) *Inspiration: Capturing the Creative Potential of Your Organisation.* Palgrave Macmillan, Basingstoke, Hants

6 Cova, B, Kozinets, R and Shankar, A (2007) *Consumer Tribes.* Butterworth Heinemann, Oxford

7 Spinoza, B de. *Tractatus Politicus.* Rendered into HTML and Text by Jon Roland of the Constitution Society (1998). Available at: **http://www. constitution.org/bs/poltreat.txt.**

8 Published in English as 'the death of the author', in *Image-Music-Text* (Hill and Wang, 1978), pp 142–48, translated and edited by S Heath

9 Harvard Business School Press (2004)

10 See *RED PAPER 01. Health: Co-creating Services,* with H Cottam (Design Council, 2004)

11 See Owen, H (2008) *Open Space Technology – A User's Guide,* 3rd edn. Berret Koehler, San Francisco

Connected individuals

06

- Understanding motivations
- Creative thinking
  - Managing negative attitudes
  - Props and cues
- A social environment
- An opportunity to participate
  - Consumers as ethnographers
  - Rewards
- Conclusion

'*The purpose (it seems to me) of human discourse should be to exchange our innermost thoughts and feelings. In other words what I'm asking is to see the* man *speaking – not the mask.'* ALCESTE IN ACT ONE OF *THE MISANTHROPE* BY MARTIN CRIMP (ADAPTED FROM MOLIÈRE'S *LE MISANTHROPE*)

In the co-creation model we will now focus in on the individuals that generate creative input, the motivations, attitudes and behaviour they bring to the process and the role of the organization in nurturing a human-centric environment. The implication here is twofold. The organization needs to see the task as an open work, where movement towards new directions remains possible and there is an explicit invitation to people to make the work together.[1] As in any successful relationship, this requires the ability to learn, to admit failings and to change. Nonaka and Takeuchi point out much of this interaction is based on what is known as 'tacit knowledge' – the direct sharing of experiences between innovators and customers.[2] In this way, co-creation can be seen as fluid and organic. The danger here is that managers close their minds. They start to believe they already know the answer to the problem and the tone of the conversation shifts to a negating of possibilities. Then there is little chance of movement; communication becomes ineffective and the opportunity for creativity is inhibited. On these occasions, people stop listening, reflecting and questioning and start telling. Similarly, individual participants need to adopt a posture of openness. If the community or event dialogue is to be rich it has to allow for multi-dimensional points of view and a sense of continuously expanding movement and meaning; the creation of the feeling that we are discovering something new both about the world and also ourselves.

When we have these conversations we can feel engaged and fulfilled and connected both to other people and the brand. The sponsoring organization enables the possibility of rich dialogue by creating a context and a positive tone to mediation, but the corporate presence should be subtle and participants should be able to take on a greater responsibility for defining the co-creation culture they are part of. For example, if we look at the way people from Danone's Activia brand community talk about their involvement, we see high levels of engagement and a sense of freedom from corporate control.

> I have come in from The Activia Advisory Board – which is an amazing community – I've made really good friends there. We talk about all sorts of really interesting things – share news, help each other with problems and also talk about Activia products.

> What surprised me? Well that the AAB is such a super place to be. !!

> I've also come from the Activia Advisory Community, I think the things that surprised me most is how well the community gelled in such a short period of time and the weird and wonderful tangents that subjects took.

> I've come from the Activia Advisory Board. I've enjoyed all the friendly banter to and fro, and am suprised how pleased I have got when someone has responded to my comments.

The interesting inference that can be drawn here is that while individuals appreciate the space of interaction created by the community, it is nonetheless a space which has to be founded and built on an understanding of their needs and motivations.

Understanding motivations

We live in participatory times. Technology has given us the means to engage with others and our desire for meaning drives us to share our thoughts, reflections and creativity. This desire is given voice by the Internet and events where we can engage with others in something we find purposeful. It seems increasingly our identities are expressed not only through what we consume but what we share: 'if I want my life to have meaning for myself it must have meaning *for someone else*.'[3] Artists, writers and film-makers have long understood this. This is how the director, Ingmar Bergman described his need to make films, 'I have an enormous need to influence other people, to touch other people both physically and mentally, to communicate with them.'[4] Now we too can enjoy influence through the films we make and post on YouTube, the entries we make on Wikipedia, the blogs we write and the contributions we make on brand communities. This is how we take part in the world. Whether these acts are transient or enduring, they give us status among our peers and define who we are and how we are seen. They can help us to realize what we might feel is a frustrated potential; to explore aspects of self that are buried or repressed. Giorgio Agamben writes, 'there is in effect something that humans are and have to be, but this something is not an essence nor properly a thing: *It is the simple fact of one's own existence as possibility or potentiality*.'[5]

How we actualize the potentiality we have does of course vary from individual to individual and context to context. Some people explicitly want to express parts of their identity that they feel unable to realize in their everyday work while some seek an outlet for their sense of creative potential and some simply enjoy the exchange of ideas. If, for example, we look at people who are part of the Mozilla community, there are various motivations connected to intellectual involvement, belief in the cause and also problem solving – a sort of hacker spirit. This is typical of the open source arena where individuals are fascinated by the challenge of working with code and crafting elegant solutions that will be admired by others. At Mozilla, there is an army of volunteers who spot, prioritize and solve bugs – a never-ending task in a code base of 9 to 10 million lines. This is highly visible work inside the organization and among the volunteers. Television monitors in the company's Mountain View offices provide a continuous update on the bug status and the volunteers also have the power to prevent the shipping of a new release if they think bugs are significant. The subversive spirit of Mozilla extends out into the marketing arena as well, such that tens of thousands of volunteers promote the brand, for free, through their own websites and networks. Asa Dotzler's view is that the success of Firefox as a web browser can be clearly attributed to this spirit: 'None of the things we did – the great features, the hard work on website evangelism, the stability improvements – none of that is as important as the philosophical component that allowed us to gather together a community of people.'

In contrast to Mozilla, the motivation to participate in co-creating ideas for *The Times* newspaper is much more explicitly intellectual. *Times* readers are not motivated by hacker culture but more by curiosity and the desire to engage in spirited conversation around what they regard as important topics. The sense of self-development derived from learning with others is the main reward. For Activia and Virgin Media, the motivation comes more from a feeling of closeness; a type of fan spirit that encourages people to

FIGURE 6.1   Motivations for engagement

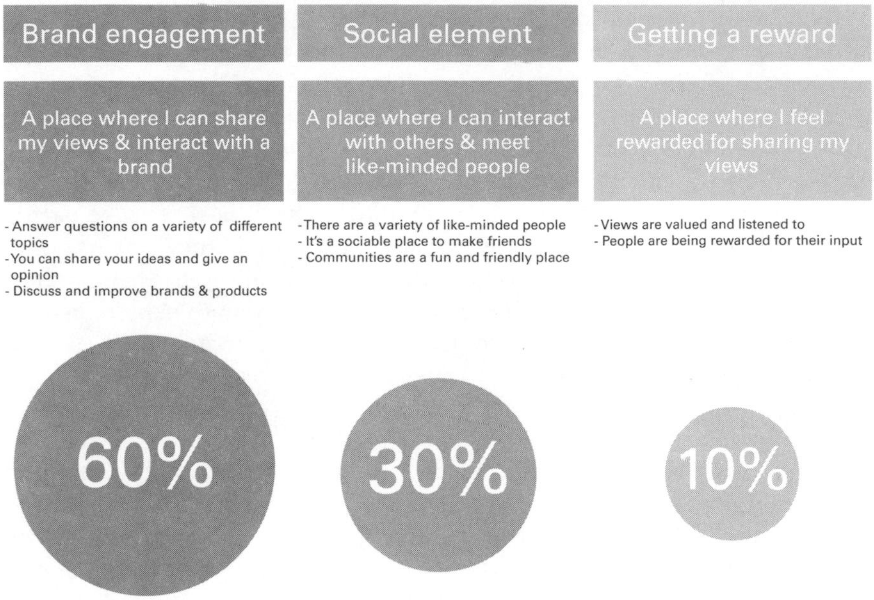

Brand engagement	Social element	Getting a reward
A place where I can share my views & interact with a brand	A place where I can interact with others & meet like-minded people	A place where I feel rewarded for sharing my views
- Answer questions on a variety of different topics - You can share your ideas and give an opinion - Discuss and improve brands & products	- There are a variety of like-minded people - It's a sociable place to make friends - Communities are a fun and friendly place	- Views are valued and listened to - People are being rewarded for their input
60%	30%	10%

want to contribute to something that they feel is their brand and forms a clear part of their personal identity. While there is a place for economic rewards in co-creation, it seems they can only supplement the much more intrinsic benefit of participation. When we asked the Brand Together community about their motivations, the rewards are mentioned by a few, but as an added extra not as the core (See Figure 6.1).

What is clear is the more the organization understands about the intrinsic motivations of the participants, the better able it is to structure the tasks, discussions and brainstorms that enable people to feel that their contributions are valuable.

Creative thinking

'Occasionally we are all stupid', writes Avital Ronell in her book *Stupidity*. We make snap decisions, we become limited by our own narcissism and we create faulty connections.[6] Even though everyone does these things, we fear looking stupid in the eyes of others – a difficulty when we consider the challenge of creative thinking where, as we venture into the unknown, the risk is increased of making premature judgements based on incomplete knowledge.[7] To overcome this fear we need an environment where we feel we can trust others; where, as Lars Nittve suggests there is 'a climate that is a safe place for ideas and where you can say stupid things, but you're not made to look stupid.' Reducing the sense of uncertainty of course takes time because it is the participating individuals themselves who need to learn to trust each other through what they say and do. But the facilitation process can make creativity more likely by nurturing a culture where interesting connections become possible and stupidity is acceptable, even valuable – for as Jacques Lacan says 'les non-dupes errent' (those not fooled are mistaken).[8] We sometimes discover new and valuable ideas through mistranslation, misunderstanding and mis-connection.

The facilitator is vital to the journey of discovery because as the representative of the organization, she or he defines the boundaries of acceptability. So, if in the spirit of encouraging people to move away from any fixed opinions they might bring, the facilitator shows a willingness to change position on a subject, it sets an example to be followed. It demonstrates a certain humanity which is reassuring and a humility which encourages participation. Some, being judgemental, might say the facilitator has undermined his or her authority, but this would be to misunderstand the role. The facilitator should be primarily concerned with creating a conversational flow by encouraging the participants to listen and be open to the ideas of each other. This helps to create a space of pyschological safety that is essential in co-creation.

When confronted by uncertain environments most of us look for somewhere safe where we can hide our anxieties. The best therapy though is to bring the anxieties out into the open, so that all the participants can see that, although they may have different concerns, there is a shared humanity. The international healthcare provider, BUPA, posed as an initial question to its community, 'what is your greatest healthcare fear?' This deliberately induces anxiety because it is very open-ended: how revealing should one be? Rather than waiting for the brave volunteer, the role of first confessor has to be taken up by the facilitator who must honestly share his or her own most deep-seated fears. This makes the facilitator vulnerable rather than venerable – a good place to be if the conversation is to progress. Once the initial difficult step has been taken and fears have been shared, the microculture of the community begins to form and people much more easily overcome their inhibitions. While participants might look to the facilitator for guidance, she or he has to avoid standing on a pedestal. The facilitator must resist the temptation to assume an omniscient role but be able to admit to not knowing things and to failings. This is a difficult balance because while the participants should not begin to question the reliability of the facilitator, on the other hand it is important for people to feel comfortable in a milieu where they don't have to be obviously smart.

The overall atmosphere that ought to emerge is positive, exciting and awash with possibilities. Johnson talks about creating an innovation arena based on 'the adjacent possible'. His argument is that ideas are 'works of bricolage', conjured out of the detritus of our lives and 'built out of a collection of existing parts'.[9] When we borrow things from different contexts and re-assemble them in new ways, we make new connections. Borrowing a line from Picasso, Steve Jobs once noted that 'good artists copy, great artists steal'. Part of the task in establishing co-creation environments is to enable this theft to take place. How can we create the tools and the attitude to facilitate people making useful links; a sort of directed serendipity? Two elements are important here. First, participants need to get rid of the negativity that limits creativity. Second they need the props and cues that help to make surprising connections.[10]

Managing negative attitudes

Herman Melville's short story, *Bartleby, the Scrivener*, features a character whose inclination is always to say no. There can often be a number of Bartlebys in co-creation processes. Participants are invited to discuss and create ideas about a brand at an event or in a community and desperate to get their long-repressed complaints heard they embark on forthright criticisms. Once one person gets on a hobby-horse, others are sure to mount up. If the group is trying to create something new, continued rejection of ideas soon generates a downward spiral. It is impossible to stop some people bringing their negativity with them but on the other hand it is possible to channel it. So rather than denying the existence of criticism, the facilitator should start by giving people the chance to rant. Ask, 'what are the three worst experiences you have had with this brand?' and then let people have their say. The challenge here is not for customers, who normally seize the opportunity to criticize, but for the participating managers who have to take the abuse and who may discover that some of the certainties that they hold sacred may be threatened. Clearly managers ought to be forewarned about this and encouraged to learn from it, too.

Guy Crawford, CEO of Jumeirah, argues that when people vent their negative feelings, often with passion, you can generate very useful insight. For example, when Jumeirah conducted a two-day event and discussed with customers the idea of value, people got very heated about paying for broadband Internet access, 'I would say that we were surprised by the depth of ill-feeling amongst some people in some of our hotels. And it was really a feeling of people saying we are already paying a great deal of money and we don't mind paying more, but please don't nickel and dime us.' Similarly, other blind spots which frustrated people, such as check-in and check-out processes, were brought to light through really listening to customer complaints. Once the negatives have been expressed, righting them together with those same customers, as in the case of Jumeirah, can become the focus of the immediate co-creation efforts. This is a powerful motivation for participants, because they not only see their opinions being listened to, but they also get the opportunity to shape the solution. The dismantling of the negatives at the front end of co-creation also serves the valuable process of allowing the ideation phase to be more positive. There tends to be less of the 'you can't do that' or 'someone else has tried that', when people have already got the negative out of the way at the beginning. Of course, this process is neither perfect nor linear. There is still the opportunity to go back and sometimes that should be welcomed if it stimulates new perspectives. Baker, Jensen and Kolb point out that conversational learning combines both linear and cyclical processes as new ideas are advanced discursively and then questioned recursively.[11]

Props and cues

A second aspect of creative thinking is concerned with the props and cues that help to shake us out of rationality and generate new connections. In the case of face-to-face events this might include using out-of-the-ordinary venues, creating a playful space, giving people things to experiment with and make things from and using performative activities. The value of play is that it spurs creativity, because 'in play, people imagine the world differently, constructing alternative frames for meaning and interaction as well as alternative forms of individual and collective identity.'[12] When we play at roles or games, we move beyond the day-to-day frames which constrain our imagination. Instead of just seeing the literal purpose of things that are defined by the language of categorization, we begin to see new, previously unimagined, uses. Rather than relying on past experience we can see objects in new ways. We can even break free of the constraint of language by creating new metaphors that bring a fresh perspective into focus and set the imagination to run down a new path. The product design consultancy, IDEO, encourages the playful exploration of connections, both through using an extensive collection of props in brainstorming processes and by encouraging employees to bring their interests and hobbies to work and use them in innovation processes. Each IDEO office has a store of interesting materials and products and curators make sure that the knowledge is shared across the different locations, such that someone sitting in Sydney can reference something in the collection in Palo Alto.

In thinking about playfulness what becomes valuable are the lateral sparks of connectivity it can create. This is thought that meanders into interesting connections through individuals following their own ideas. As Deleuze and Guattari playfully suggest, 'if thought searches it is less in the manner of someone who possesses a method than that of a dog that seems to be making uncoordinated leaps.'[13] Helping uncoordinated leaps to happen ought to be part of the co-creation process. Participants in events need to be encouraged to journey beyond their normal experience and online communities should have the opportunity to create their own discussions and brainstorms – indeed on the Brand Together community there were more than 100 brainstorms initiated by participants ranging from 'can you remember what you watched as a child' to 'brainstorm boredom' to 'infidelity'. Rational managers might see all this as purposeless and in terms of relevance to the organization

FIGURE 6.2 Poll from the Brand Together Community: 'I feel the Community allows me to be creative!'

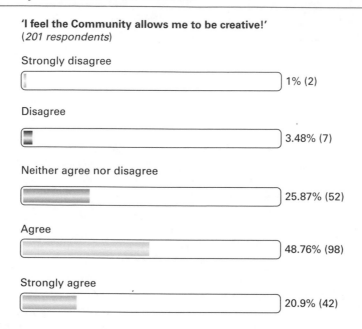

'I feel the Community allows me to be creative!'
(*201 respondents*)

Strongly disagree

1% (2)

Disagree

3.48% (7)

Neither agree nor disagree

25.87% (52)

Agree

48.76% (98)

Strongly agree

20.9% (42)

some of it might be. However that is hardly the point. For play to be play it cannot be overly instrumental. Play is about discovery and the opening up of adjacent possibilities which might drive a new way of seeing a problem or finding a route to a solution. It also has a clear impact on those involved and the way they see themselves because play helps to generate a feeling of creative potential (See Figure 6.2).

A social environment

One of the strong motivations for many community and event participants is the sociality of belonging. This is clearly fundamental in naturally occurring communities where the impetus for starting and sustaining a group comes from the individuals who are enthusiasts for a particular brand. In these communities the something in common is the sharing of a world based on the meaning that the brand generates for the members. It is a specific instance of togetherness. Kornberger writes, 'branding does not try to manipulate aspects of life. Rather, through the regime of lifestyle, brands become ready-made narratives about oneself, society and culture . . . branding structures how we behave as consumers and how we engage with society as a citizen.'[14]

In other words, we should not see participation with brands as somehow additional to everyday life, but as a fundamental part of our being-in-the-world. When we apply this thought to organization-sponsored communities, we need to be more cautious. It is no longer the case that individuals have sought the community, but rather that it has come to them. If belonging comes to be significant because it taps into existential needs, then people may start to engage in conversations and tasks. On the other hand, the community may not deliver on the expectations and then people can become passive adherents and contribute little. This indicates that while the community is an entity with a culture of its own, it offers different things to different people. At one level community members see the purpose as functional. It is concerned with sharing, but it is also clearly about creating value for the organization. This comment from a Brand Together community member is a typical interpretation of this perspective in that the community is described as an object separate from the subject:

> The community is a place to share ideas with other members to help improve products or give thoughts/ideas about future products. The purpose is to help a company design products that the consumer wants.

Yet, it is clear that for some a community can come to be much more: an emotional touchpoint that is clearly ontological and focused on the joy of connecting with others. Here the language is one of inclusion:

> It's a web site that I can log into whenever I want to, and I am able to read the thoughts and comments of other community members. It's quite good as you can have a conversation about something that can span over days, and just contribute to it when you have time, or when something pops into your head that you want to add to it.

> The community facilitators do set you questions and tasks to respond to, and they send you an e-mail to tell you that you are needed on site. These questions/ topics are usually quite interesting and that bit is enjoyable as you put your own opinion and then read the opinions of others – choosing to point out something that you don't agree with if you feel you want to.

> The Community is really very friendly – there are lots of different types of people in it and we talk about all sorts of things on the side pages in between official topics. If I had a particular shrub or plant for my garden that I didn't know how to care for, I would post a question for all to see and the members reply to my question with any advice that they have.

> We also have a lot of fun – there are quite a few people in the community with a 'special' sense of humour, it's these people that get some really interesting/ diverse topics going that we all join in with and it keeps us all amused – AND keeps us all logging into the site at our own will rather than just when we get the official request.

> The best thing about the community that I am a member of is that it is relatively small so you tend to get used to the same names popping up and actually get to know the people a little bit.

It's a great place to while away those spare minutes that you find through the day. We also get an incentive each month which isn't a huge amount but all the same feels like a gift when you get it. Most of us save our incentives in our on-line accounts and buy ourselves treats or save towards Christmas gifts.

Most of all the important thing is that it is what it says, A COMMUNITY !!!

The capital letters of 'A COMMUNITY' and the three exclamation marks indicate its fundamental importance. In this quote, it is clear that the tasks, while interesting, are not the primary motivation – but rather the sense of being linked with others, sharing thoughts and lives and creating a community. This feeling of closeness can be described as a form of social capital, the informal values and norms that permit cooperation between people. Francis Fukuyama describes the components of this form of capital as 'truth telling, meeting obligations, and reciprocity'.[15] If there is a lack of social capital, trust diminishes and the community ceases to be functionally effective. When social capital is strong, however, it powers the connectivity between people, allowing them to make jokes, join in banter and discuss the plants in the garden. This reinforces the point that successful communities are valuable for those who live within them not as an instrument of corporate will but in their own right. We might ask then what the benefit of this is to the organization? Surely talking about aspidistras or yuccas is not much use to a bank or a fast food chain? Yet this is to miss the point. The groundswell of positivity generated in a community permeates all discussions. By enabling the community to talk about what it deems important, the social capital created facilitates a more fruitful discussion of interest rates or hamburgers. To think in a purely instrumental, rational way about communities is to misunderstand their essence. Creative thinking and innovation happen among people because of their capacity to interact with each other. It is the drive of the singularities in a community that realizes creativity. As Kozinets *et al*, observe, 'Collective consumer creativity. . . occurs 'when social interactions' trigger new interpretations and new discoveries that consumers thinking alone, could not have generated.[16]

An opportunity to participate

It seems evident that the very act of participation can be meaning-making. When asked about their experiences of interacting with brands, the Brand Together Community members stress the satisfaction and stimulation that comes from being connected to others.

While this group is very positive, we should note, however, that not everyone will feel energized by an event or a community. Some people are more misanthropic than others and may dislike the principle of sharing thoughts and emotions. Others, especially non-customers, may find the category or brand out of tune with their interests. Whatever the causes, participation levels will vary. Some enthusiasts will be active while some

FIGURE 6.3 Participants recognize the benefits of the online community experience

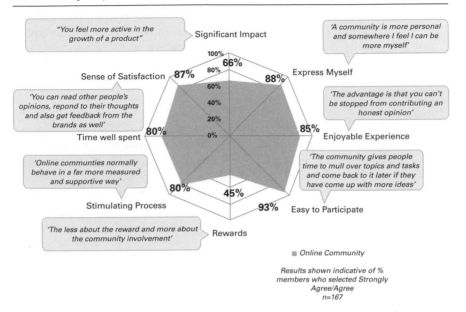

cynics will barely register. The likelihood of active involvement generally increases when people feel that what they are involved with is of interest and somehow valuable to others and to the organization. These judgements are always individual but it is possible to heighten interest and occasionally to surprise people by taking them into areas they had never previously considered. Spurred on by interesting stimuli, we can suddenly find we are excited by The Clash or new product development in soft drinks:

> I have come from Sony Music Backstage, I was surprised to be invited to that community because of my taste in Music. . . its amazing what you learn I hadn't realized most of the artists I enjoy were part of the CMG catalog. Not long after joining SMBS I was invited to become an insider and write a weekly blog. I really enjoy this and would miss it if they ever stopped it.

> I'm from TATA – have been a member there for a long time – really enjoyed all the different things we ended up thinking about – some really odd!

If, as Schau *et al*, suggest, 'participants derive social and hedonic value from the experience' of brand-centred communities, then everything from the initial invitation to the after-event feedback should tap into this.[17] Generating interest clearly starts with an exciting FBQ, but it also requires a language that is inclusive and actions that stress the valued status of the participants.

Consumers as ethnographers

In the case of Orange, the communication of the importance of those contributing began with the initial briefing. Orange recruited four different teams of consumers comprising two teams of trend setters and two who fitted the profile of the target audience. The teams were then invited to a briefing meeting where they were told about their task; to generate a game-changing innovation based around the idea of relationships for a mobile communications provider. They were to be ethnographers for a week and a half, observing their behaviours, interviewing their friends with their mobile phones and mapping the nature of their relationships. After this initial stage the teams were brought together again and debriefed. The third stage in the process was a two-day, large group event where all the teams plus a control team participated in developing ideas and presenting them. It was only at this point that Orange was revealed as the sponsor of the process and the teams then assessed whether what they had developed aligned with the Orange brand. It's easy to imagine that when trust is given in this way and people are asked to be actively involved throughout the process from observation to idea generation and development that they feel a sense of fulfilment. Nick Bonney observes that the Orange managers who participated in the event were surprised by how the teams engaged and how passionate people were about their ideas. The words 'passion' and 'energy' are often used by managers to describe co-creating consumers.

The point we should absorb about the Orange process is that consumers are likely to be highly motivated by a task such as this which is seen to be important, challenging and fun. That again means trusting people and being transparent and honest with them. To nurture this requires a tone of facilitation that encourages self-belief. Take for example the invitation to the Brand Together community to take part in an innovation challenge. The tone is conversational, the task seems exciting and there is a specific commitment to make use of the ideas. See the next page.

The detailing of the process, although long, is also important because it helps to reduce the level of anxiety about what is expected. Not surprisingly the response to the invitation was very positive with people using such words as 'great', 'challenging', 'scary', 'fantastic', 'intense' and 'interesting'.

> This is a biggie isn't it?! Will have to make sure I think very carefully – it's good to be so involved – and to be instrumental in something that could actually happen!

> Mmmmmmm! This IS a challenge – I understand that we are looking to create a marketing/communication tool rather than a product. Let's go for it. . .

Rewards

People engage with brand communities and events mostly because of the opportunity for meaning-making and socialization. This can surprise managers

Introducing the innovation challenge!

Dear community members!

A few of you have been asking what the last phase of the brand together community is all about: please find a summary of everything you need to know below!

First of all some good news: due to your fascinating contributions and the overall success of this community, we would like to extend it by one week and of course we would love you to stay around until the end (naturally we will keep our promise and reward everyone who has taken part in 12 official activities or more at the beginning of next week)!

After we have asked for your feedback and opinions in the last few weeks we would like to use the remaining time to really try something new: we would like to invite you to co-create and invent something together – something that is new and that hasn't been done before. It's not going to be easy, but then you are an amazing crowd to try and do this with!

Our brief

As you know, we at Promise are all about engaging consumers and employees in co-creative and collaborative activities to help companies become better companies. All of you have seen how we use online communities to help us do this. Now we would like to work with you over the next two weeks to invent the future of co-creation!

We will be discussing questions like these:

What new types of activities could we be designing?

How could we truly revolutionise the platform we are currently using?

How can we engage and excite citizens and consumers like you even more?

How can we create more interaction between you and our clients?

We don't know yet what the solution will look like, but we know that we won't be able to do this without your help.

Why should you care?

There are at least two reasons why this might be interesting to you: firstly we pledge to actually implement at least one of your suggestions on our platform. Your input will make a real difference to how we co-create in the future. Secondly, there is a realistic chance that Prof. Nick Ind – who has been reading a lot of your comments throughout – will include some of your ideas in a forthcoming book about co-creation (he is keen to make the point that everyone can be creative and invent new things, not just the 'experts'). So if you want to end up in a widely published book with your idea and your name next to it, this is for you!

(continued)

FIGURE 6.4   The Brand Together community innovation Challenge

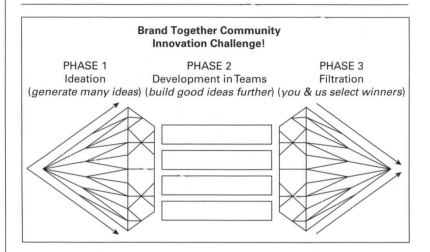

The innovation process will have three different parts (please see the diagram, too):

Phase 1: Ideation

> We will launch an innovation brief today and will create the 'ideas room' for you to post any ideas and suggestions you might have. It's a new type of activity we have created a few months ago. You can review each other's ideas and vote for things you like best.

Phase 2: Development

> Monday we will take the best ideas that have been created in the Ideas Room and will define a handful of teams that will each develop one idea further (of course we will help you with this!). The idea is that by the end of development we have a good understanding of what the new concept is trying to achieve and how it might look.

Phase 3: Filtration

> Finally, by the end of next week, we will put all developed ideas into a format where you can vote for new ideas other teams have developed and we at Promise will put together a jury, reviewing all of your ideas. After this we will have a final list of winning ideas – and we promise that we will implement at least one of them in the next 6 months!

Please let us know in case you have any questions – we are happy to help!

Best,

Lilli

who tend to assume that financial incentives are vital for participation. The rewards element is clearly secondary for most people. Yet it should not be ignored. There is always the possibility that the reason for people's involvement can tip from joy to disillusion if they begin to feel they are being manipulated. Financial rewards help people to rationalize why they participate and also provide a monetary benefit for their time and commitment. Normally rewards are given on the basis of participation and in the form of vouchers. But as well as these financial incentives we should note the other form of reward for participants; being listened to by brands they like and admire. This sense of contributing to how a brand may develop or communicate (as we saw with the example of *more!*) is an emotional reward that makes people feel much closer to the brand. The important point here for managers to note is that this places an obligation on the brand owner to be active listeners and to give attentive, continuous and prompt feedback. Having given of themselves intellectually and emotionally at an event or in a community, participants expect the organization's members and the facilitators to reciprocate by demonstrating the impact of the contributions received.

> I would like to see our opinions really having an effect on clients and the brands we are going to be discussing. Amazon vouchers are great but big companies listening would be even better.

Conclusion

Co-creation participants are motivated by a variety of factors that range from creative expression to a quest for meaning to socialization. When organizations understand these motivations and can tap into them with engaging and involving processes, then people can begin to feel a strong sense of involvement and ownership. Individuals become willing to reveal their whole selves and expend their time and energy creating something valuable for the organization and themselves. While the organization creates a framework for innovation and can nurture the microculture of the community or event, we should note that co-creation is clearly about the relationships that develop between involved individuals. The temptation with a company-sponsored co-creation process is to attempt to control it; successful co-creation requires managers to let go of their brand and let people mould it for them. When teams have this freedom and responsibility, as we saw with the example of Orange, then they rise to the challenge while generating meaning. One final word of caution here. As people begin to feel such a strong connection with the brand they are helping to co-create, it becomes vital for the organization to keep the involvement going by providing feedback on how ideas are developed and a conduit for further discussion. Co-creation participants feel the need and they also have the potential to be very powerful brand evangelists.

Notes

1 Eco, U (1962) 'The Poetics of the Open Work' in *Participation*, ed Bishop, C, pp 20–40, Whitechapel and The MIT Press, London and Cambridge, Mass

2 Nonaka, I and Takeuch, H (1995) 'Organizational Knowledge Creation' in *Creative Management and Development (3rd edition)*, ed Henry, J, pp 64–81, Sage Publications, London

3 Blanchot, M (1998) *The Unavowable Community* (La Communauté Inavouable), Les Editions de Minuit, 1983. Trans. Joris, P, p 22, Station Hill, Barrytown, New York

4 Singer, I (2007) *Ingmar Bergman, Cinematic Philosopher: Reflections on His Creativity*, pp 27–28, MIT Press, Cambridge, Mass

5 Agamben, G (1993) *The Coming Community* (La communita che viene) Enaudi, Turin, 1990. Trans. Hardt, M, University of Minnesota Press, XI, Minneapolis

6 Flaubert once wrote in a letter, 'stupidity lies in wanting to draw conclusions' (la bêtise consiste a vouloir conclure).

7 Google even celebrates 'stupidity' – the Penguin Award, as it is known, is given each year to someone who took a chance 'but messed up big time'. Similarly Tata also has a Dare to Try award, 'which encourages people to come up with ideas that are genuinely different – an acknowledgement that you have to be prepared for something not to work at all if you want it to make a big difference.' Chynoweth, C 'Dare to try, the Indian way', *The Sunday Times* 17 April 2011, Features.

8 Zupancic, A (2008) *The Odd One In: On Comedy* p 85, The MIT Press, Cambridge, Mass

9 Johnson, S (2010) *Where Good Ideas Come From: The natural history of innovation*, Allen Lane, London, p 35

10 An interesting example of this is the set of cards created by musician, Brian Eno and artist, Peter Schmidt (1996) known as 'Oblique Strategies – over one hundred worthwhile dilemmas'. Eno described the cards, which feature provocatively oblique phrases, in an interview in 1980: 'The Oblique Strategies evolved from me being in a number of working situations when the panic of the situation – particularly in studios – tended to make me quickly forget that there were other ways of working and that there were tangential ways of attacking problems that were in many senses more interesting than the direct head-on approach.' Brian Eno, interview with Charles Amirkhanian, KPFA-FM Berkeley

11 Baker, A C, Jensen, P J and Kolb, D A (2005) 'Conversation as Learning Experience.' *Management Learning* 36(4), pp 411–27

12 Statler, M, Roos, J and Victor, B (2002) 'Ain't Misbehavin': Taking Play Seriously in Organizations.' *Imagination Lab Foundation*, 28, p14

13 Deleuze, G and Guattari, F (2003) *What Is Philosophy?* (Qu'est-ce que la philosophie? 1991). Trans. Burchell, G and Tomlinson, H, p 55, Verso, London

14 Kornberger, M (2010) *Brand Society: How Brands Transform Management and Lifestyle*, pp 198–99, Cambridge University Press, Cambridge, UK

15 Fukuyama, F (2000) 'Social Capital' in *Culture Matters*, Harrison, L and Huntington, S P eds, Basic Books, New York

16 Kozinets, R V, Hemetsberger, A and Schau, H J (2008) 'The Wisdom of Consumer Crowds: Collective Innovation in the Age of Networked Marketing.' *Journal of Macromarketing* 28 (4), p 341

17 Schau, H, Jensen, M, Albert, M Jr and Arnould, E J (2009) 'How Brand Community Practices Create Value.' *Journal of Marketing* 73 (5), p 31

The co-creation toolkit

07

- Discovery
  - Art from Within
- Ideation
  - Imagibuild
- Development and filtration
  - Developing and filtering at Tata
- Conclusion

'Inventive work in fact seems to consist in an endless movement towards, into, around and away from a problem. . . It is repetition, *we might say, but of the attempt. . . What is at stake is not closure but the opening out of further possibilities.'* **THOMAS OSBORNE, 'AGAINST CREATIVITY'**[1]

In this chapter we will look at the space of co-creation where the organization and the connected individual meet. Whether this is an online or live encounter or a mixture of the two, the important thing is that both sides are prepared for the experience. Organizational members must have a clear understanding of the FBQ and the process they are going to undertake. They also must have relinquished the idea that they are somehow separate from the consumers and other stakeholders they are about to meet. Their attitude must be one of equality; a part of the co-creation team on a level footing with external participants. Above all they must be open. The connected individuals that will come together and share and learn from each other need also to be well briefed about the project. They should have as much information as they need to perform the task and they should know what is expected of them and feel safe and confident. The task of the mediator is to nurture these attitudes and to steer the agreed process while being attuned to the need to adapt it where necessary. In *Brand Together* the space of connection and conversation is presented neatly as an ellipse where the organization and participant meet but it is in fact always changing as ideas jostle and meanings move. If it appeared in a comic, it would have ((( ))) around the shape to suggest the sense of movement.

Within the moving space – and indeed part of the reason it is fluid – are the various processes that are designed to elicit engagement and creativity. While the toolkit of possible interactions is extensive, we will focus in this chapter on some of the key ones that are involved in discovery, ideation, development and filtering. Here we should emphasize that no one tool is better than another in itself, but rather that they are appropriate to different contexts. Deciding which tool to use at which point does depend on the task in hand, but it is also a question of judgement as to what is likely to be most effective. The important unifying factor in the tools and the way they are used is to generate the involvement of the maximum number of participants in the most insightful way. To illustrate the use of the different tools, we will both describe the idea behind them and also how they have been applied in co-creation projects. In online processes – as we saw in the last chapter with the Brand Together Innovation Challenge, the different phases of innovation can be worked on continuously by the same group of people. Sometimes this can be condensed, but also the process can stretch over several months, especially if prototypes need to be developed, sampled and discussed.

Outside the digital world, the main focus is on events. When the task is specific and contained, the core process can be focused around half-day participatory workshops. Typically these would involve a limited number of consumers and company managers working together to solve a specific issue. When the innovation task is bigger and perhaps looser, the better format is large-scale groups across two days. For example, when Etihad used the process to look at the design of the interior of the new Airbus A380, each group comprised approximately 40 consumers, 5 experts (designers), 3 senior managers, 5 staff and 5 facilitators. Having two days meant people could not only discuss past and present experiences but also envision the future and then build physical prototypes of the in-craft experience. Neither the workshops nor the large groups are necessarily isolated events. The process may require people to participate in several sessions as ideas evolve and similarly the early stages of discovery and ideation, which face-to-face is particularly suited to, can then flow into a community which might become a permanent fixture in the organization's co-creation armoury. Whether the organization opts for a one-off project or the adoption of co-creation as a way of life depends on the philosophy adopted. As we saw in Part One of this book, in this regard organizations range from the experimenters to the enthusiasts.

To represent the flow of innovation, the traditional model is a funnel, where a large number of ideas enter, are developed and then a few selected

FIGURE 7.1   Four phase model of co-creative innovation

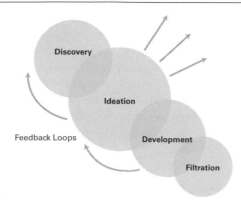

for final testing. The funnel suggests a one-way flow, however, and it is clear that innovation processes are messier than that, with backward flows as ideas are revisited and reworked. IDEO's Tim Brown in presenting the concept of design thinking uses a circular model that allows for backward movement. In this approach everything links from inspiration to ideation to implementation in a continuous loop.[2] The iterative model, in which he cites the inspiration of Edison, has the virtue of connecting everything, but it misses out the active involvement of both client organizations and customers as co-creators. Consequently it presents a very valid rationale for the expert-led approach but lacks a sense of openness. In Figure 7.1 we show an alternative perspective on the innovation process that incorporates the together element and builds on a preparatory phase that is concerned with generating focus inside the organization and ensuring that the right stakeholders are engaged and well-briefed. The phases of innovation are:

1 **Discovery.** This phase involves discovery of the world, the brand and oneself. It looks outwards to find and anticipate change and it looks inwards at the attitudes and motivations of those coming together and the emerging microculture of the community or team. This part of the process leads to the discarding of some aspects of discovery and a focusing in on those parts that seem to be important.

2 **Ideation.** This phase opens out the innovation process to explore the boundaries of adjacent possibilities to imagine what might be. It absorbs the lessons of discovery to create a departure point for the group. It may include visualization and fast prototyping techniques.

3 **Development.** Lars Nittve likens the innovation process to an accordion. If ideation is the expansion of the accordion, then this is its contraction. During development important ideas are reviewed and taken deeper to explore their potential and their limitations.

4 Filtration. The final phase prior to implementation is the selection of the final idea or ideas. These may be subject to validation through traditional testing and quantitative research. The relevant stakeholders, whether consumers, partners or employees should ideally be involved throughout the process. This helps to ensure a continuous orientation on the needs of stakeholders. If the community or team is closed (limited to those people invited to take part) then it is also possible to pause at any point and to validate ideas through wider engagement. It is also an option to open the process up, to create, for example, public design competitions where anyone can participate.

Two further things to note about the model. First, the series of feedback loops and centrifugal arrows indicate that although the model does have a direction it is possible to revisit earlier assumptions and to challenge the boundaries. As Delanda suggests non-linearity defines 'a world capable of surprising us through the emergence of unexpected novelty.'[3] Secondly, models tend to both reveal and conceal. This model reveals the integration of stakeholders from the very start of the process but it also tends to conceal the fact that both the organization and participants bring a whole set of experiences with them. This is one of the reasons, mentioned earlier, for tackling the past before considering the present or the future. It suggests that the shapes of the model sit within a sea of chaos; as if the tidy circles of a constructivist painting were placed in the middle of abstract expressionist drips and traces.

Discovery

Before a co-creation process begins there has normally already been some discovery work. The initial research, interviews and discussion have begun the journey of discovery for the organization. In setting the FBQ and the boundaries for creativity, insight has been generated on the most important segments for the organization to target and the problem that has to be resolved. In this phase, the organization begins to reach some sort of consensus on what it believes it knows and where its uncertainties and blind spots lie. There is also the emerging self-discovery of managers as their beliefs and ideas are challenged, negative areas defined and new positions emerge. Discovery suggests we need to be both attentive to things that perhaps have escaped our observation before and willing to move to new understandings. This makes journey and relationship-mapping particularly useful exercises because they provide an insight into the lived experience of customers as they interact with the brand rather than a company-centric view (See Figure 7.2).

Similarly, the individuals who are going to take part in co-creation need to be willing to open themselves up to new experiences and to better

FIGURE 7.2   Example of relationship map

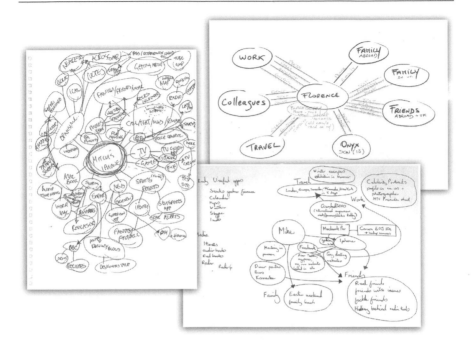

understand the world around them through the sort of ethnographic approach that Orange undertook and also through exercises that aim to bring their own deeper feelings to the surface. This is a key element of the co-creation idea because it argues that the way we interact with brands is not mainly about the rational, surface-level articulation of likes and dislikes but rather the senses that we have that are rooted, hard to elicit and voice. Jean-Luc Nancy reminds us here that sense is a word with a double meaning. It identifies the process by which we sense something through our faculties and it is also 'the sense, the thought, the universal underlying the thing'. Yet as Nancy points out, these two meanings have the same sense because the meaning of the word is derived from the passage of one into the other.[4] In other words to get an idea of what something really means we need to move from the sensory to making sense. One of the key tools here is known as Art from Within.

If we are asked to describe a brand in words we immediately become troubled by the intrusion of rational thinking and also the inadequacy of language. We are stuck with a limited vocabulary, which partly explains why the same words keep appearing in brand vision and value statements. These words often only become adequate to the task once they are given a narrative context that determines their real meaning for the organization.

To get round the problem of language, one technique that researchers have long employed is to ask participants to express their understanding of the brand metaphorically: what if brand x were an animal? What if brand y were a car? This does provide another layer but while knowing the brand is a tiger or a snake offers some sort of insight for the researcher, it gives very little sense of discovery for the participant. The idea of Art from Within is that it offers a journey of discovery for the individual and the organization.

Art from Within

The concept of Art from Within derives primarily from Surrealism. Influenced by Freud's thinking on visual imagery concerning the 'emotional attitude' behind intention, from the 1920s onwards a loose group of poets, artists, writers and film-makers became interested in exploring the creativity beneath the surface of life. The core principle was that the unconscious was the real source of imagination but that it was hidden and repressed by a rational approach to the world. Rather than being expressive, people succumb to the desire to normalize and categorize. The Surrealist answer to this was to try to release the unconscious by negating the effect of conscious reflection. The writer André Breton argued in his *Manifesto of Surrealism* (1924), 'It is true of Surrealist images as it is of opium images that man does not evoke them; rather they 'come to him spontaneously, despotically. He cannot chase them away; for the will is powerless now and no longer controls the faculties.' The strategy here is not to try to think one's way out of a dilemma but instead to take advantage of the accidents and ideas that just happen. For example, the German artist Max Ernst tried to use chance as an artistic principle. He would take a pencil and make a rubbing of a textured surface – whatever appeared he would either leave or use as the basis for further development. Alternatively he would paint and then scrape away the surface to reveal the form underneath. Schmied describes the process as 'a continual exchange of impulses between the subconscious and conscious mind, enabling the artist to mobilize all the hidden resources of his visual imagination by systematically surprising himself.'[5] Similarly, the French artist André Masson experimented with automatic drawings – doodles of personal images inspired by chance and drawn quickly without aforethought.

The inspiration of these surrealistic techniques can be applied to the innovation arena as a means of reaching beyond the rational to create surprise and insight. The typical context here is a brand that seeks to better understand itself and its place in the world and participants who are interested to deepen their sense of the brand as part of their journey of discovery.

The Art from Within technique asks people to present their idea of the brand through drawing. It can take the form of asking people to draw the positive and negative side of a brand or a current feeling or a sense of the future. The important aspect of the task is to reflect the surrealist approach by doing the image quickly and spontaneously, avoiding as far as possible the effect of conscious reflection and enhancing the possibility of happy accident. As with all these processes, the facilitator should demonstrate the task by making a drawing first. This is both a chance to illustrate the speed with which the drawing should be done and to demonstrate that artistic skill is not the important element. Once the drawings are complete, the artists should be asked to explain as best they can what they have drawn. People usually find Art from Within tasks enjoyable if sometimes embarrassing.

Nonetheless it generates two important benefits. First, it starts to bring to the surface some of people's more deeply held motivations and feelings they may not have expressed before. In the act of drawing, new insights as to the role of the brand in their lives start to emerge. Second, Art from Within creates the opportunity for people to tell a story about their relationship with a brand. Rather than the static image that is often created when people try to summarize verbally the essence of their perceptions, drawing enables them to narrate an evolution: 'when I started drawing I was thinking x but as I continued I noticed y and this made me realize z.' Communicating this sense of movement also draws in comments from the facilitator and the other participants which both deepen and broaden the meaning.

Ideation

While discovery is often focused on the present or the past, pinpointing problem areas and creating a focus for innovation, the ideation phase is clearly future-oriented. Here everything is possible. So whereas perhaps the boundaries of creativity are narrowed during other stages, in ideation boundaries should be wide and subject to challenge by participants. This is the phase of positivity. For the time being issues of resources, competencies and acceptance can be put to one side in a search for ideal solutions. We can take inspiration here from Google's approach to innovation. Jan Grønbech of Google says that there is a philosophy in the company that all possibilities can be explored: 'no project is too big or too small. At Google there are two questions it is forbidden to ask: Is this economically feasible? And is this technologically possible?' The argument is that many of Google's success stories were neither technologically possible nor economically feasible when they were conceived, so these should not be ideation barriers. The evolution of ideas as they are developed from conception creates the possibility to realize the seemingly impossible. Also as technologies change, ideas that may have seemed far-fetched suddenly become achievable.

Ideation can be conducted online, as attested by the numerous open innovation challenges that companies organize, and as the Brand Together community demonstrates, but it is perhaps more powerful when it is sited in a face-to-face event. There are three reasons for this. First, there is the galvanizing power of challenging tasks that help to focus a team working together. Second, events create specific opportunities for interaction in the form of role-play and the construction of space. Third, it is easier to provide the prompt material that can spark off interesting adjacent possibilities. Yet, whether ideation is online or live, we should remind ourselves that it is not conjured out of thin air. Choosing the right individuals, creating a worthwhile task, enabling learning, engendering trust and making space are necessary antecedents to idea generation. The quality of creativity is determined by how well the group itself builds its own sense of entity. Anton Ehrenzweig reminds us that the relationship between the singular individuals within the group is itself creative in that it requires generosity, humility and a lack of envy. Individuals have to be able to give part of themselves to others and be able to take back the additions to the self given by other independent personalities. When this flow between individuals emerges it extends the knowledge and capabilities of all concerned. For example, if one individual has a specific idea and relates an experience, other members of the group can absorb the experience and add to it, through an additional narrative. As long as people are receptive, the initial thought can zig-zag in new directions and deliver surprising insights far away from the initial thought. Where this fluidity breaks down is when individuals feel unable to accept the ideas of others or the development of their own ideas in unanticipated ways. What we should be working towards here is to move ideas from individual to collective ownership. It is the idea that matters, not its progenitor: 'to accept the work's independent life requires a humility that is an essential part of creativity.'[6]

While the departure point for creativity may be based in memory and experience, we hope that the end point takes us somewhere fresh and new. This is hard to achieve because there is the undoubted temptation to adapt what we have done before – and indeed these insights can also be valuable. In the group work for Orange, for example, one of the reference points for young people taking part was Blackberry Messenger – an instant messenger application used as a means of social networking – which had never been really noted before by Orange managers. When it comes to ideas beyond the range of experience, we need to engage in what the writer Coleridge called primary imagination: 'an act of creative perception through the mind, in which the images are generally fresh and original rather than derived from memory.'[7] Here we confront a problem and rather than searching our bank of experience to adapt something we have done before, we re-frame the challenge and create new ways of seeing. When we get stuck in what Coleridge called 'fancy', which he equates to drawing on memory, we seem to keep hitting barriers that constrain our line of flight. The best way to attain primary imagination is to free ourselves. As Ginger, leader of the would-be escapees, says in Aardman Animation's film, *Chicken Run*, 'The fences aren't just around the farm. They're up here, in your heads.'[8] The best strategy to enable escape is to encourage the group to explore extreme possibilities. Whereas individual thoughts are easily limited, it is possible for a group to create ideas that move beyond individuality into collective invention – something that Johnson sees as the norm in innovation from the Industrial Revolution onwards.

Imagibuild

One of the tools for imagining the future is a group-based activity known as Imagibuild. The important principle here is that the group has the opportunity not only to imagine but also to build. This sense of bodily engagement is valuable because often thought can only take us so far. We might ask, 'how would it feel to be insecure in your home?' or 'How does it feel to sleep on a plane?' but language only gets us to a surface level. We might talk in the former case about fear, anxiety and connectivity, but it can be hard to imagine ourselves into the situation and know what we would really do. It is only when we act and experience what we have imagined that we realize the real possibilities. The philosopher, Maurice Merleau-Ponty stresses the importance of our bodily engagement with the world, because he argues that we do not so much think our way into action, but rather that we act our way into thought, such that the body is not an object of the world, but our means of communication with it.[9]

If we were to ask a group to build 'the future of ocean cruising' we might ask the groups to design the most important spaces and services, while considering the following questions:

- What should the experience be like?
- In what way would it be different from now?
- How would it help people like you?
- How would it fit with the brand?
- Who would it appeal to?
- How could it be promoted to consumers?

To tackle this challenge, the group might construct spaces, create artefacts, develop collages, design advertisements and perform role-play. The active part of the process is designed both to liberate creative thought by generating new possibilities through the act of making and to create a focus for the actions of the group. When you have a physical object or space the group can walk around it, study, reflect and suggest improvements. Here we not only get an idea of the practicalities of the thing that has been created but we can begin to feel what it is like to be in a space and to understand how the often idealistic values of a brand can be translated into something tangible. The possibility of experiencing an environment also means that whatever the group creates can be shared with other groups in the room, drawing in their ideas and inspiring their creativity.

CASE STUDY   [yellow tail]

[yellowtail] is an Australian wine, owned by Casella Wines. Launched in 2001, the brand now sells over 12 million cases in 50 countries. In the USA, it became the number one imported brand within three years of launch. Such was its rapid success that Chan Kim and Mauborgne featured it as a case in their 2005 book, *Blue Ocean Strategy*. They argued that by ignoring the snobbery associated with wine brands and by focusing on a new segment of non-wine drinkers, the brand redrew the strategic profile of the US wine market: 'it didn't simply steal sales from competitors; it grew the market. [yellow tail] brought non-wine drinkers, beer and ready-to-drink cocktail consumers into the wine market.'[10] Yet, [yellow tail] is not a typical success story as we might find among the strategic planning schools of deep analysis and prescription. Rather, like Absolut vodka, it is a story of intuition, creativity and emergent strategy. John Casella's family company had long been in the wine business both in Italy and then Australia. His aspiration was to move away from supplying other brands to building his own. The philosophy, which is perhaps a reflection of Australian culture, was to make a wine that was approachable and accessible – something that everyone could enjoy. As a symbol of that the company adopted a stand-out name and graphic (a yellow footed rock wallaby) which had nothing to do with wine heritage but a lot to do with Australia and the tone the company wanted to adopt. Marketing manager, Libby Nutt, describes the launch:

> we did a lot of analysis, looking at the US market and trying to find a niche in what was already a crowded market. John Casella was adamant that we needed to be in the right price corridor and getting that right has contributed to our success. As has the quality and consistency of the product and the quirky bright packaging that helped to demystify wine buying. It was pure intuition that guided John.

Having used intuition at the beginning, the question emerges whether you can keep doing so. Casella did have a feel for its customers' attitudes and behaviour, but when it came to re-thinking and re-vitalizing the brand and exploring whether it could innovate in new ways, the company wanted reassurance and direct input. [yellow tail]'s use of co-creation seemed both culturally appropriate and a good way of tapping into the passion of customers. Starting in Spring 2011 and working with both current and potential customers, [yellow tail] conducted half-day discovery and ideation workshops in the USA, Canada and UK. These were designed to provide an insight into attitudes to consuming wine and other beverages; to help in understanding people's emotions towards the brand; to generate communication concepts; and to direct innovation efforts. Key to the process was to select the right people and then to prepare them by asking them to write a love story about [yellow tail]. Treated sceptically, this could become a parody but it is clear the participants took the idea seriously. The preparatory work helped ensure that people were already engaged with the brand when they arrived for the workshops. The stories surprised because of what they said about the extent of the participants' brand literacy generally and their insight into the [yellow tail] brand personality specifically. For example, these two fan stories demonstrate the imagination of the writers and their ability to position [yellow tail] in their own worlds.

> [yellow tail] is a classy lady. She's young, but worldly and from a distant land. She hangs with common folk. She is fun, energetic, young at heart, and wouldn't let me spend too much money on her. But, Miss [yellow tail] and I are only friends. She's a free spirit. Houston fan.

> How do I feel about [yellow tail]? Just the thought of it takes me back to picnics for two in the long grass, getting away from it, a feeling of loyalty and trust. . . no other wine really compares. London fan.

In the workshops, with fans, potential customers and [yellow tail] managers all working together, a series of activities was designed to draw out deep-seated feelings about the category and the brand. In the discovery phase journey-mapping and Art from Within techniques were used. The journey-mapping process was insightful because it continued the love theme, showing how customers are seduced by the brand from the first social encounter to enjoying the taste and the experience to a relationship based on good memories and a sense of fun. The cues that are employed in each part of the journey also reflect, a bit unnervingly, how personal relationships can evolve. In the initial phase the cues are largely physical in the form of the label, the Wallaby and the associations generated by Australian-ness (which are not the same in all markets). In the wow moment, it is more the product attributes that matter, such as the smooth taste, good value and consistency. Finally, in the last phase, people adopt a regressive state of mind. Stimulated by the visual identity, they can enjoy a Proustian moment[11] as the taste of the wine transports them back to an earlier occasion of enjoyment.

In the Art from Within exercise, the idea was to explore the meaning of [yellow tail] and to gain an insight into consumers' rational and emotional attitudes towards the brand. Libby Nutt says, 'initially going into it I was really intrigued by what would come out of it and I was wondering how consumers would be able to express themselves. And I was really astounded by how they talked about it and what came out of it was fascinating, actually. I think for some people it is a much easier way to express themselves rather than just through words.' Sometimes Art from Within generates images and themes that are very similar, but as a reflection of the diverse impulses connected to the brand and the different stages of maturity in the markets, the [yellow tail] pictures provide a broad base of insight.

Mirroring the journey mapping process, some of the pictures evoke similar themes. For example the image of child-like fun is a rejection of the traditional attitudes to wine which is related to old-world products, grown-up occasions with rituals and the fear of right and wrong. The sort of scenario that features in the film *Sideways* (2004) as wine connoisseur Miles and lothario Jack take a road trip through the wineries of California. At a wine tasting, Miles explains the ritual:

> Miles: Let me show you how this is done. First thing, hold the glass up and examine the wine against the light. You're looking for color and clarity. Just get a sense of it. OK? Uhh, thick? Thin? Watery? Syrupy? OK? Alright. Now, tip it. What you're doing here is checking for color density as it thins out towards the rim. Uhh, that's gonna tell you how

FIGURE 7.3   Art from within examples

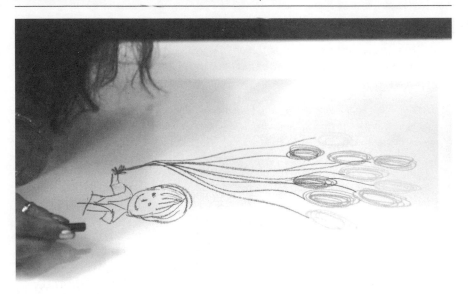

old it is, among other things. It's usually more important with reds. OK? Now, stick your nose in it. Don't be shy, really get your nose in there. Mmm. . . a little citrus. . . maybe some strawberry. . . [smacks lips]. . . passion fruit. . . . . . and, oh, there's just like the faintest soupçon of like asparagus and just a flutter of a, like a, nutty Edam cheese. . .

Jack: Wow! Strawberries, yeah! Strawberries. Not the cheese. . .

Miles: Are you chewing gum?

With [yellow tail] customers there is no soupçon of asparagus or flutter of nutty Edam. Rather the occasion is the thing. It creates a sense of childlike freedom, free of ritual: a wine there to be enjoyed with others in a fun atmosphere.

Where these two exercises come together is in providing inspiration for ideation, both in terms of creating suggestions for a new brand platform and generating proposals for brand innovation. [yellow tail] is clearly not Miles with his pretensions, but neither is it the decadent Jack – although it is far closer to his down-to-earth, 'tastes pretty good to me', and fun-loving attitude. As Nutt says of the US customer base for [yellow tail], 'they don't really care about regions or wine-speak.' The ideas that were developed bring this sense of everyday accessibility, fun, authenticity and sociability to life. In particular, the strong idea of the brand that emerged during the workshops fuelled people's ideas about exploring new directions for [yellow tail], such as sauces, marinades, clothing and beer.

Interestingly [yellow tail] had already discussed the possibility of a beer brand, so the endorsement from the workshops gave the innovation an added fillip. Libby Nutt says of the workshops that the aim was to unlock insights and get close to customers. Her view is that when the discussion became more technical, such as on packaging formats and

FIGURE 7.4   New product ideas developed in the [yellow tail] workshops

sizes, the co-creation process was less productive but that when it came to brand insight and more thematic innovation, it was powerful in releasing creativity: 'it was really interesting to see how the consumers opened up without being worried about the clients in the room and how they really had lots of thoughts about the brand – what they liked and didn't like and how to fix it. It was insightful just to be part of that process.'

Development and filtration

The two elements of development and filtration are combined here, not because they are the same but because there are large areas of overlap and they often occur simultaneously. In the development phase, ideas that have been pitched during ideation are selected and then evolved. In the process of evolution it becomes clear that some ideas cannot be realized, do not meet business needs or are inappropriate for the brand. At various key points concepts will be evaluated against a checklist and either filtered out or given the go-ahead to proceed to the next stage. There may also be more formal market research conducted and also market testing. Finally a concept, or maybe more than one, will make it through from its original conception to market realization. The danger here is that the more bureaucratic the process, the slower and potentially more compromised the innovation will be.

Although innovations rarely, perhaps never, make it through from original idea to execution untouched, the more hoops there are to jump through, the greater the likelihood the idea will deviate from its intention or never happen. A study by Michael Kirton of the way ideas are developed in organizations found three main barriers. First, the involvement of managers from different departments results in long delays in introducing change. Second, ideas get blocked by a series of well-argued and reasoned objections, which are then supplemented by a critical blocking event. Third, ideas that are put forward by managers who are unacceptable to an 'establishment' group are subject to opposition and delays.[12] Luckily there is also subversion. For example, Virgin Group have a motto: 'screw it, let's do it.' Their argument is that if you spend too long thinking and analysing an idea you will probably have missed the opportunity. Similarly Google and open source businesses are willing to move rapidly to testing in the market place. The principle is simple – if the idea is good, the nature of networks will determine rapid adoption; if it is nearly good the network will suggest improvements. Finally, we can subvert by using co-creation to involve managers from different departments throughout the process and by using the power of direct consumer contact to overcome received ideas and 'reasoned objections'.

Given the tendency of innovations to be emergent, what becomes clear here is that, while the original spark of creativity that generated a concept is central, innovation must embrace all the small pieces of creativity that help to realize it. Ed Catmull reminds us of this when he narrates Pixar's approach to creative development: 'A few years ago, I had lunch with the head of a major motion picture studio who declared that his central problem was not finding good people – it was finding good ideas. Since then, when giving talks, I've asked audiences whether they agree with him. Almost always there's a 50/50 split, which has astounded me because I couldn't disagree more with the studio executive. His belief is rooted in a misguided view of creativity that exaggerates the importance of the initial idea in creating an original product. And it reflects a profound misunderstanding of how to manage the large risks inherent in producing breakthroughs.'[13] The implication is that it is in the nurturing of a group of people who collectively can deliver an idea such as *Toy Story* or *Cars*, that innovation can be found. This requires a mixture of what Kirton calls innovators, people who are more likely to reconstruct a problem and separate it from the accepted way of doing things, and adaptors, people who are better at taking existing problems and solutions and working within constraints.[14]

Developing and filtering at Tata

The online world is particularly valuable in idea development. In some cases ideas will migrate from live events, but also some organizations brainstorm their own ideas and then ask a community to develop and filter. For example, Tata Global Beverages wanted to develop a new drinks concept that would align with its declared vision of creating 'life-enhancing sustainable hydration'. In other words drinks that are enjoyable and can have a positive environmental impact. Tata first of all posited a problem which was that a lot of the negative impact with soft drinks was due to the transportation of the water content. This led to concepts based around a concentrate that water could be added to. The company felt this was a good solution and a good message but when the ideas were put to the online community that had been established, the feedback on the environmental positioning was overwhelmingly negative. Mark Putt of Tata says, 'they (the community members) understood why those things were important but they were not a key driver of purchase. So we had to look for other propositions and other ways to express the benefits of this product. And the communities enabled us to do that.' The community members however did like an alternative concept and gave suggestions as to how that could be developed. At this stage Tata recognized that consumers had to have something tangible to interact with so six different positioning platforms were created and prototypes of the product were produced and sent to customers in their homes for adults and children to experiment with. Putt argues that not only did this produce clarity over how to proceed, but it helped to persuade people inside the organization: 'we could show videos of children with a webcam at home filming themselves interacting with the product for the first time and that real fresh moment of consumer excitement. And that became a very powerful part of selling the idea internally because the immediacy and the potential of the idea came across very well in those little vox pop moments.' Additionally managers also had the opportunity to take part in two Livejams, where, in a moderated process, people discussed the concepts and how they could be positioned. For Putt this was an epiphany. Unsure whether people were going to come back to the community and contribute, he was surprised by the constant stream of ideas. Putt is clear about the value of online communities: 'as far as developing ideas is concerned, screening ideas and looking at a broad range of things very quickly, I think this is a great methodology.'

The Tata example typifies the complexity of decision-making. Building an innovation around a clear vision statement would seem a sensible step because it brings life to the vision and provides a narrative to support the idea. However, while 'sustainable hydration' was motivating internally and a supporting argument externally, it became obvious in this case that its use in a product would not be the primary cause of purchase. For customers (and especially children), the important aspect was the novelty of the product delivery and the taste experience. This hints that the real issue in the development and filtration phase is enabling the organization to distinguish between 'the important and the unimportant, the relevant and the irrelevant. A well-posed problem gets these distributions right, and a solution always has the truth it deserves according to how well specified the corresponding problem is.'[15] The interviews conducted with managers for this book echo this theme because people often argue that many of the ideas that emerge from co-creation have at one time or another been voiced within the organization. However, managerial myopia means that certain problems are not seen as sufficiently important or relevant to be emphasized. It means that some ideas and opportunities are missed – witness 'guitar groups are on the way out, Mr Epstein'.[16]

As well as the iterative approach described above it is also possible to democratize the process of idea filtration. Companies might like to be more directive and make the final decision about which ideas to pursue but the virtue of asking people to discuss and vote on ideas opens up the process and indicates which are the most important ones for them. In the Brand Together community members posted more than 200 ideas. As many of these covered similar ground they were then grouped into eight themes by the facilitators and then the ideas were voted on. This helped to generate focus while still providing the opportunity for 'expert' adjudication on the idea(s) with most saliency. Another, and perhaps more dramatic, device is to use a Dragons' Den process; the tool Barclays and Orange used to filter ideas. As the approach is derived from a popular television series it already resonates with people and needs little explanation. The competitive spirit that it imbues is also seen as exciting. The desire to be the creators of the chosen idea helps to glue a team together and to extend themselves beyond their perceived potential. Organizations are often surprised by how much passion people bring to this process but for the participants there is the excitement of being part of the theatre of a reality show format.

CASE STUDY   Felix Koch describes the key principles of online co-creation

Ten ideas for building a vibrant online co-creation community

The objective of this section is to provide a set of ideas that will enable people to curate successful co-creation communities. It is worth mentioning though that not all flourishing communities will have lived by these rules and neither will the implementation of these inevitably lead to great communities. Nevertheless these building blocks are based on having run over 25 co-creation communities over four years. The order of the guidelines is loosely based on the chronology of setting up, running and finally closing co-creation communities.

The ten ideas for building a vibrant co-creation community have been written with the following scenario in mind:

- there is a public or private sector organization with an innovation, insight or strategy challenge

- there are a few hundred participants (consumers, citizens, employees and/or other stakeholders) who have been invited to collaborate on this challenge

- there is a facilitating party who sets up and manages the online community

You will notice that none of the ideas cover the technical question as to what kind of online platform to use. While web-based platforms have made co-creation communities possible, we believe that more often than not people get too hung up about features and functionalities. A few core tools like member profiles, facilitator features and the ability to post comments seem essential, beyond that, **soft skills tend to beat software**. When implementing the ideas below the question as to whether you use an online forum, a be-spoke community platform or even just a Wordpress blog, becomes secondary.

Before we start, a word of encouragement. None of this is rocket science. We all understand how to engage with other people, how to create a sociable environment and what it takes to be a **good host**. All we really need to do is to think about how *we* would like to be treated and what would encourage *us* to participate in a mediated collaboration exercise.

Idea 1: Define the higher purpose

What is the objective of the community? What topic or challenge unites every single member? Think of online communities like a **barn raising event:** we want participants to focus on a specific task and we want them to work together on it as a team. Define very carefully and in very simple terms the barn you are trying to raise and think about what participants would find most motivating. Typically, a higher purpose might revolve around inventing the future of an organization/category or around solving a meaningful challenge a brand/company is facing. Make the community invitation as big as possible (while still being able to deliver on it!). Without a common goal or a shared journey, a community is not a community.

Idea 2: Set the ground rules

Communities are the result of careful social engineering. To create a successful com-munity it is important to **define the rules of engagement at the beginning** and to do so in a very clear manner. When participants join the collective they will have all sorts of questions on their mind. What is this community about? How long is this community going to exist? What is my role going to be? What are the values of the community? Who is responsible for running it? What do I get out of it? Who else is here? What is acceptable behaviour? In communities the small things are not the small things. Define your values and the rules of your community using a tone of voice suitable for your participants.

Idea 3: Encourage diversity

A diverse community will be more engaged, creative and productive than a homogenous community. **The best ideas and the biggest breakthroughs will come from unexpected places** and the speed of idea generation and problem solving will be much higher if par-ticipants from different age groups, backgrounds and experiences build on each other's ideas. Think about the audience you want to engage and the different groups that have a stake in the challenge at hand. Some segments will be more difficult to recruit than others but do your best to develop mechanics that will interest and engage participants beyond the obvious target audience.

Idea 4: Relationships are the source of results

We will only get people's full passion if we help to create relationships between community members. Typically, this process should take place in the initial phase of the community called **warm-up** (maybe the most neglected aspect of setting up communities). Before we can engage participants with the actual challenge/topic at hand, we need to introduce them to each other and to ensure that they bond as much as possible. The beginning of any new community is hence characterized by activities that make participants open up and share something personal (the facilitator of course often goes first to make things easier). This is no psycho-babble but the basis on which all future community phases are built. The more community members share and get to know each other during warm-up, the more they participate and the deeper the insights.

Idea 5: Foster interaction

The explosion of the social web is establishing a new paradigm of empowerment and interaction. Top-down is challenged by bottom-up and the monologue of those in power is being replaced by conversations between equal participants. Online communities are flagship examples of these developments. Facilitate as much peer-to-peer interaction and conversation as possible. Allow community members to comment on each other's ideas and communicate amongst themselves in private. **Give them the tools to ask their own questions and enquiries**, don't be scared by the wealth of data this will generate! Similarly, encourage interaction between the sponsor of the community and its participants; the more these parties interact the better and the more robust the outcome will be.

Idea 6: Make it fun and creative

Being part of a community should never feel like work or an onerous chore. For two reasons it should rather be entertaining and playful. First of all community members who enjoy the activities and challenges **will participate longer and more frequently**. Second, the community **will generate more and better ideas** if they are given the opportunity to express themselves through a range of tools (rational and emotional, creative and analytical). Keep the interest of community members high by introducing new activity types and mechanics such as competitions, team exercises, picture or video based tasks.

Idea 7: Praise and reward your community

To keep participation and engagement high throughout the lifetime of the community it is important to develop a bespoke reward and incentive model for each community. Think about your audience. What type of people do you want to get involved and what would drive their participation? The answer will vary depending on your target community and may include drivers such as **access to insider information, peer recognition, intellectual stimulation, monetary incentives or working for a good cause.** Apart from the overarching participation strategy, it is important that the community facilitator rewards individual behaviour as well. Praise individual contributors publicly and do so in a specific, personal and authentic way.

Idea 8: Share as much as you can

Ask community members why they take part in online co-creation and the ability to have an impact on the challenge at hand and the sense of making a difference by sharing ideas usually ranks at the top of the list. To satisfy these key drivers of participation you need to be prepared to share as much about the progress of the project as possible; the influence of the community; the new products, services or campaigns affected by or even developed by community members; the reasons why certain ideas have been rejected. **The principle of reciprocity** is central in keeping community members engaged. Let the community know why you are asking the questions you are asking, introduce them to the client organization and its inner workings and provide them with a roadmap of the time ahead.

Idea 9: Provide closure

When the challenge at hand has been solved, sometimes a community comes to an end. Once the barn has been raised everyone goes home. **However, it is important to give as much thought to how to end a community as you would do setting it up.** From the roadmap community members should have a good understanding of when the community might come to an end. Before that date make participants aware of the fact that the community is closing down and explain why. Provide an overview of past successes and the impact the community has had on the sponsor organization. Explain what will happen next with the results. Many people will have invested a lot of time and emotional energy into your community; treat members with respect and provide time and space for people to say goodbye. Detailed feedback activities can often help. What has worked really well? What could be improved next time round? What was the best/worst moment on the journey? Keep the community open for a bit longer and allow people to exchange details if they wish to stay in touch.

Idea 10: Break the rules

Finally you need to be flexible. Very flexible. Online communities have not been around for long and are constantly evolving organisms. What has worked today might not work tomorrow. Technology changes as does the way in which humans use technology (just think of the explosion of smart phones). So it pays to adopt an 'always in beta' mindset. With every community try something new. Do the exact opposite of everything written down in this section. Play with all the variables; use more people, fewer people, change the incentive system midway, discourage diversity. And keep learning how to best engage, motivate and stimulate large groups of people.

Felix Koch is Consultancy Director, Promise Communities

Conclusion

Jean-Claude Carriere says, 'A work of art isn't created a masterpiece, it becomes one.'[17] For ideas to develop beyond their original conception they have to be developed creatively and they have to be successful in the marketplace as they are purchased and used. Consumers and other stakeholders can and should be involved throughout the process. In this chapter we have tried to demonstrate how that can be achieved from discovery through to ideation and then development and filtration. What results may not always be radical innovation, but that generally neither surprises nor disappoints managers. The battle inside the organization is most often not about originality of thought, but about exposing the obscured; a bringing into the light of the most important and relevant ideas for consumers. The co-creation process is designed to achieve this by tapping into people's emotional relationships with brands and helping them to draw, build and write what this means for them within the context of a safe and trusting environment.

Notes

1 Osborne, T (2003) 'Against 'Creativity': A Philistine Rant.' *Economy & Society* 32(4) pp 507–25

2 Brown, T (2008) 'Design Thinking.' *Harvard Business Review* 86(6) pp 84–92

3 Delanda, M (2002) *Intensive Science and Virtual Philosophy*, Continuum, London, p 155

4 Nancy, J-L (2002) *Hegel: The Restlessness of the Negative*. (Hegel: L'inquiétude du négatif, Hachette Littératures, 1997.) Trans. Smith, J and Miller, S, p 46, University of Minnesota Press, Minneapolis

5 Schmied, W (2006) *Francis Bacon, Commitment and Conflict*. Trans. Ormrod, J, p 83, Prestel Verlag, Munich, Germany

6 Ehrenzweig, A (2000) *The Hidden Order of Art*. p 105, Phoenix Press, London

7 Bohm, D (2004) *On Creativity*. pp 50–51, Routledge Classics, London

8 Ind, N and Watt, C (2004) *Inspiration: Capturing the Creative Potential of Your Organisation*. p 60, Palgrave Macmillan, Basingstoke, Hants

9 Merleau-Ponty, M (2002) *Phenomenology of Perception*. (Phénomenologie de la perception, 1945: Gallimard, Paris.) Trans. Smith, C, p 106, Routledge Classics, Abingdon, Oxon

10 Chan Kim, W and Mauborgne, R (2005) *Blue Ocean Strategy: How to Create Uncontested Market Space and Make the Competition Irrelevant*. p 31, Harvard Business School Press, Boston, Mass

11 In Proust's *In Search of Lost Time* everyday experiences, such as tasting a madeleine biscuit are capable of taking someone back to the past as the sense is stimulated and connected to earlier associations.

12 Kirton, M J (1984) 'Adaptors and Innovators: Why New Initiatives Get Blocked.' *Creative Management and Development (3rd edition)*, ed Henry, J, pp 109–19, Sage Publications, London

13 Catmull, E (2008) 'How Pixar Fosters Collective Creativity.' *Harvard Business Review* 86(9) p 65

14 Kirton published a method for scoring people's adaptive and innovation propensities in the *Manual of the Kirton Adaption-Innovation Inventory* (1977), National Foundation for Educational Research, London.

15 Delanda, M (2002) *Intensive Science and Virtual Philosophy*. p 127, Continuum, London

16 Decca Records response to The Beatles manager, Brian Epstein, having heard the group play on 1 January 1962. Instead Decca signed Brian Poole and the Tremeloes, who had auditioned on the same day.

17 Carriere, J-C and Eco, U (2011) *This Is Not the End of the Book*. (Ne pensez pas vous débarrasser des livres, 2009. Éditions Grasset & Fasquelle.) Trans. McLean, Polly, pp 159, Harvill Secker, London

Branding together with other stakeholders

08

- Creating together with partners
  - Client focused innovation at First Data
  - Rabobank's high participation culture
- Creating together with employees
  - The benefit of a participative approach to brand definition
  - Web jams at IBM
  - How Kraft Foods co-created its purpose and values
- Creating together with citizens
  - Involving citizens in tax compliance
- Conclusion

When asked by the English film director, David Lean, 'What kind of crew do you use?' the Swedish director Ingmar Bergman replied 'I make my films with eighteen good friends.' Lean replied, 'That's interesting. I make mine with 150 enemies.'[1]

In this chapter we will move away from the focus on customers to explore how organizations co-create with citizens, professionals, partners and employees. However we immediately encounter a problem of definition. Surely co-creation is the norm with these other stakeholders? Bergman made his films with his 18 friends as they came together and shared ideas and expertise. Even Lean's 150 enemies somehow managed to work together and co-create epic films. Similarly organizations enter into joint ventures with each other to create new offerings, suppliers work with companies, sometimes in long-term relationships, to solve problems and employees participate in teams on innovation projects. It is impossible for businesses to remain separate from the world. They have to work with outside expertise and they have to use the skills and knowledge of employees to create intellectual capital. To make sense then of the term co-creation in the context of these other stakeholders, we need to be more specific about what we mean. There would seem to be two key points differentiating co-creation here that link back to the original idea presented in Part One.

First is the attitude that pervades the relationship to other stakeholders. The film director might be an individual who works and evolves ideas together with friends so that everyone contributes to the creativity of the piece (much like at Pixar) or he might be someone who imposes his will on others and thereby constricts the opportunity of team members to contribute creatively. The position the director adopts is defined by the attitude to participation – either he believes in the creative contribution of others or he simply sees people as the instrument of his will as 'auteur'. Cultures in businesses can also be supportive of the principle of participation by adopting a participatory market-oriented philosophy that involves employees, customers and other stakeholders in the development of the brand. Here managers help the organization to become participatory by investing in processes that encourage high levels of connectivity with stakeholders.

Second is the principle of openness to others. When the organization believes it has most of the answers it is likely to be more introverted. If, alternatively, it possesses humility, it is more likely to make a conscious effort to seek out interesting and valuable partners that can help to enhance its brand. BMW's Palo Alto office epitomizes this spirit. BMW set up its office in 2000 to co-create new ideas within the Silicon Valley ecosystem; to have direct contact with lead users; to absorb influences from partners and to work with emerging software and electronic technologies outside of the traditional automotive arena (see YF Juan on A Silicon Valley Perspective). Stephan Durach of BMW says, 'we learned very quickly that we had to have an open network to get access to and to share information and also that we needed to build prototypes to prove viability in the automotive context.' The two-way flow of information and involvement with big companies such as Apple and Google, start-ups, venture capitalists and academic institutions such as Stanford, Berkeley and UCLA is generated through personal connections and network meetings. Durach points out this exploration of ideas could never be managed out of the headquarters in Munich because so much of the work is based on personal relationships, 'the initial contact is much easier here. . . it is a lot about networking and trust building. . . and being open.' There is also a clear value for BMW in learning by doing. The development of relationships needs to be rooted in the practice of making concepts tangible through prototyping. This has led to innovations such as the first automotive integration of Apple's iPod (when many other manufacturers were still focused on compact discs) and Google's 'send to car', which provides in-car navigation. It is BMW's willingness to engage with others and to be receptive to the world around it that enables it to co-create.

Creating together with partners

Many companies have long practised a form of co-creation with their business partners as together they create tailored processes and products. Yet the emergence of online communities and the growing complexity of many areas have resulted in a sea-change of creativity 'into something rich and strange'.[2] Increasingly companies come together with other quite diverse organizations to produce innovations. P&G has become a strong advocate of this open innovation philosophy as its markets have moved from slow predictable change to 'very rapid change, elimination of geographical boundaries, remarkable global capabilities, and constant focus on lower costs.' AG Lafley, then Chairman and CEO of P&G, set a target in 2001 that 50 per cent of innovations would involve an external partner – a target that was reached in 2007. For P&G, collaboration can involve diverse partners: 'P&G likes *un*-usual suspects.'[3] We can also see this more open philosophy emerging in financial services as the industry becomes more focused on technology. For example, the creation of Google Wallet – an application that allows people to use their mobile phones to conduct credit and loyalty card transactions – brings together mobile phone operators together with Google, First Data, Citi and MasterCard. Each partner brings a different set of skills and knowledge. Similarly, Rabobank, which has strategic partnerships with Microsoft, Oracle and Cisco, also owns its own mobile phone company.

Client focused innovation at First Data

First Data, a US-based merchant processing services business, has deliberately tried to become more connected to its customers. With larger businesses it identifies problems and opportunities, as it has long done, and co-creates solutions through one-to-one relationships. The process here is a simple one of regular dialogue over time that enables First Data managers to identify with its clients' issues and work effectively. It is a natural way of doing business. What has been added is an ongoing online community of small merchants. This is a closed community of invited participants that helps First Data to co-create and evolve new products. John Elkins, President, International Regions, says that the payments industry 'has become a hotbed of innovation because of regulatory changes and also because of the capabilities offered by new technology. That is spurring us to embrace co-creation as an input.'

For Elkins, the danger of technological innovation is that it encourages a business to push technology at clients rather than taking into account their fundamental needs and then using technology to meet them. The community is the antidote to this tendency. It helps to ensure that innovation is relevant and usable. We might observe, relative to a consumer community, that the attitudes and motivations on both sides are slightly different. For the small merchants there is little of the hacker or fan spirit. The interest is largely professional in that the participants are motivated primarily by the desire to help shape products and services that are beneficial to their businesses. There may also be some add-on value for individuals both in terms of the social aspect of the community and the opportunity to learn from, and with, others in similar spheres, but these tend not to be core. Also, while consumers can be surprisingly revealing about themselves, in business communities there is the sense that one should not strip oneself bare. There is then sometimes a holding back and a focus on what seems to be essential. This helps to reduce the meandering one sees in consumer communities, that is useful for adding texture but sometimes takes people off in very different directions. Similarly the circumstances are somewhat different for the organization. Given the explicit and often long-term interdependence of the company and its clients, there is an added responsibility to listen carefully and ensure that feedback is given. We would argue that this responsibility also applies within the consumer field and that when organizations ignore it, they do at their peril, but business-to-business relations are, if anything, stickier. This is why both sides need to work hard to realize the opportunities generated through the community.

Rabobank's high participation culture

At the Dutch-based Rabobank there is a similar commitment to creating with partners. Indeed it is part of the heritage. Rabobank is a cooperative bank with its roots in rural communities. It now has nearly 60,000 employees and some 10 million customers in 48 countries. One of the things that distinguishes the bank is its inverted structure. In the Netherlands there are 141 independent Dutch Rabobanks which are governed by locally-appointed members. The local banks steer the facilitating and connecting role of Head Office in Utrecht, especially in non-banking activities.

In the last 10 years the local banks have got bigger and now employ on average around 300 people. This means they wield more power and have acquired their own specialist experts who operate at the local level. Given the strong sense of being community builders among the Rabobank branches, there is a rich heritage of co-creation among the highly participative members, through informal dialogue, local member councils and member events, which the head office helps to facilitate by providing a platform where people can discuss important issues.

Branch management teams have to explain their strategy, services and finances to the local members and it is the members who help to decide how the dividends paid into the community should be spent. The virtue of the inverted structure is that it brings the managers and staff of each one of the 141 Rabobanks into close contact with members, customers and partners. This proximity and shared interest helps to generate a high-trust culture where people are willing to experiment. For example, when one branch decided it wanted to use video communication to service its partners and customers, it worked with a local IT company to install the system. Once the idea had proven to be successful other branches came to visit to see how people were being given advice via webcams. Other branches have decided to extend their reach by setting up service offices in libraries and training librarians in offering financial services advice. Maarten Korz, says there is a downside to this swell of innovation in that ideas are often reinvented in local branches but that 'giving the local branches the freedom to experiment helps the company to see how tests work and to argue things through. . . it's not about the innovation team telling them what to do, they experience the benefits themselves.'

To the traditional process of direct interaction at the local level, Rabobank has added social media as a mechanism. Through both public and proprietary tools Rabobank is encouraging members and customers to contribute and develop ideas and to help ensure that initiatives are shared more effectively between branches. Korz believes that the cooperative heritage helps people in adopting online tools, partly because 'in the offline world we are already very close to our customers' and partly because the basis of trust enables sharing. The sense of cooperation also makes it easier to build partnerships. As well as the strategic partnerships with large IT companies, Rabobank works with very small innovation companies such as the Utrecht-based Headcandy, which develops smart wall interfaces, and with Universities and Research Institutes to explore the trends of the future. Korz says that more and more of the knowledge the bank acquires is shared externally on the premise that the more you share with others, the more you get back. This hints at one of the key facets of creating together with partners for it inevitably reveals the organization and its culture and processes. That can be unnerving for an organization not used to sharing and working in this more open way, but if the philosophy is in your roots, as it seems to be at Rabobank, it makes co-creativity much easier to adopt.

Creating together with employees

In a post-Fordist world, employees are often expected to be active participants in their organizations. People take part in process discussions, project teams and brainstorming exercises. They engage in conversations with each other and they create value for customers. Indeed the very idea of organization implies the involvement of people with each other in a collective environment. Yet we can observe that organizations can be more or less participatory and that when it comes to the process of branding, their own people are often excluded. In this section, therefore, we will focus on how some organizations define and manage their corporate brands participatively.

The rationale for participation in the brand definition phase is twofold. First, given the dominance of services in most OECD countries and the principle of service dominant logic,[4] it becomes clear that branding must be an organization-wide process. Everyone, either directly or indirectly, is involved in creating value for stakeholders. In traditional thinking branding is conflated with marketing, but here branding is concerned with creating some kind of coherence around what the organization does (in terms of how and what it produces) and says (in the form of individual and collective communication). It involves business leaders, people working on product development, human resources managers, customer service personnel and also marketers. It seems clear from this perspective that the individuals who deliver the brand ought to have an active involvement in the way it is defined and delivered. Second, one of the challenges in articulating a corporate brand ideology is generating attention. Talk of visions and values can be met with a yawn, especially by those who feel that it has nothing to do with them. The distance created is often exacerbated by the definition method adopted. The approach in some organizations, which is also advocated by several writers, is that a select group of high-level people – some of whom have a marketing or communications background – are tasked with getting to the essence of the organization. They may conduct market research, consult employees and use consultants to craft the output, but the creation of the brand is determined by them. The prime argument in support of this approach is that more widespread involvement leads to woolly definitions that are insufficiently distinctive. By using experts an idea can be honed that will resonate with staff. This is a fallacious argument and it creates problems of implementation.

The benefit of a participative approach to brand definition

The value of a corporate brand ideology is that it is actually used. Collins and Porras made the point in their comparative study of 18 visionary and excellent companies and 18 merely good companies that all of them had a core ideology but the visionary companies had something more, '. . . this is the key point – they have had core ideology to a greater degree than the comparison companies in the study.'[5] What is important is not so much creating clever articulations, but rather uncovering what is true to the organization and its future aspirations. The counter accusation could be made here that what you end up with then is a lack of distinction in the words used to define the organization. However, this need not be the case in a well-planned process and the point should be made that the words chosen acquire their real meaning not at the point of articulation but by context as they are used by people in their day-to-day work: 'terms are defined within a particular context and this context changes as people construct different empirical hypotheses. The terms then take on a different meaning.'[6] Many organizations use, for example, such words as 'quality' and 'innovation' but for each organization the words mean different, and always changing, things.

When the definition has been determined by an elite group, it then has to sell what it has produced to the rest of the organization and explain why a particular choice of words might be valuable. If the articulation has been determined by the people who will use the brand, it both ensures that the ideology is representative of the whole organization[7] and begins to cement the idea through self-discovery. Participants don't need to have the brand sold to them, they already understand it: 'Far more persuasive is an approach that focuses on participation, and that works with developing the culture of the organization. Tools become the means to enable learning. The goal should be to engage employees as much as possible on a journey of self-discovery, both for themselves as individuals and as members of a system.'[8] The participatory approach enhances the likelihood that the brand ideology will actually come to mean something for people and be used in decision-making. Certainly, brand definitions are limp when no one uses them.

If we believe in the principle of corporate brand co-creation, then the issue becomes more one of the practical management of a process of collective involvement. In the past the emphasis was clearly on live engagement through teams and workshops. Organizations such as Unicef, The Economist, Patagonia and Baxter Healthcare adopted processes that involved large numbers of individuals working together to define the essence of the organizational brand. This enabled different voices to be heard as the ideology evolved through direct interaction. The challenge here, especially with globally dispersed organizations, was that conducting brainstorms around the world could be very time-consuming. Baxter, for example, took two years to define its three core values. So in addition to face-to-face events, online has created an added dimension.

Web jams at IBM

In 2003, when IBM decided to review its corporate brand values, it undertook a comprehensive values process. Three hundred executives took part in discussions and 1,000 employees took part in focus groups. These conversations helped to articulate some ideas, but as CEO Sam Palmisano notes, this wasn't enough: 'we couldn't have someone in headquarters sitting up in bed in the middle of the night and saying "Here are our new values!" We couldn't be casual about tinkering with the DNA of a company like IBM. We had to come up with a way to get the employees to create the value system, to determine the company's principles.'[9] That way was a 72-hour web jam, to which all employees were invited to contribute their views and ideas. This generated some 10,000 responses and involved not only the employees, but key managers and Palmisano. The process didn't radically alter the ideas that had been developed on the values in the initial discussions although it did help to nuance them and there was a lot of debate 'about whether IBM today is willing and able to live them (the values)'. This helped to ensure that the company paid attention to the implementation process.

Buoyed by the success of the values web jam, IBM subsequently conducted an InnovationJam that involved IBM employees, family members, universities, business partners and clients from 67 companies. During the two 72-hour sessions, participants posted more than 46,000 ideas as they explored IBM's technologies and how they could be used to help solve real-world problems and capture emerging business opportunities. IBM announced in 2006 that it was investing $100 million over the next two years in developing the 10 best ideas from the InnovationJam. Not surprisingly the theme of 'trust' again emerged as a key success factor; Palmisano noting, 'Collaborative innovation models require you to trust the creativity and intelligence of your employees, your clients and other members of your innovation network.'

How Kraft Foods co-created its purpose and values

Another organization that has combined live and online tools is Kraft Foods, the second largest food company in the world with an annual turnover of $50 billion and a workforce of over 140,000. The company was owned by Altria, (formerly Phillip Morris), until 2007, when it became an independent public company. This change, combined with a new CEO and the acquisition of the biscuits business, LU, brought with it a new strategic direction and a renewed emphasis on growth. Although the company enjoyed good margins there had been a lack of real consumer focus and an under-investment in its brand. The need to re-wire the organization and to re-frame how consumer value could be best created, led to a feeling that Kraft ought to review its purpose and values. Of course, the company could have opted for an expert-led process, but as Perry Yeatman, Senior Vice President, Corporate Affairs, observes, employee expectations have changed: 'they want to be engaged and they want to contribute their creativity.' The decision was taken to open up the discussion and to involve both consumers and employees. However, this was not without its challenges. With the change in direction and new ownership there had been reorganization and downsizing, so employees were feeling vulnerable, while managers who had been used to a very controlled environment were now being asked to let go and become transparent and participative. Yeatman argues, 'There was a lot of trepidation, so how we did the work was as important as the result.'

In an eight-month process of discussion and creation, some 10,000 employees took part in live and online events. While Kraft Foods already had a lot of brand research it became clear that there were a lot of unknowns in terms of how consumers saw the category. In the discovery phase the main mechanism was to conduct large group events in key locations (Chicago, Paris and Shanghai) where managers, staff and consumers came together to answer some core questions: how did people relate to food? What did they think about Kraft Foods products? What did they know about the Kraft brand? As with other processes discussed in this book, the participants were highly passionate in engaging with these questions. While there was some variability of response in the events (in Chicago, the headquarters of Kraft Foods, people knew the brand well, but in Paris there was very limited awareness), some common themes emerged; most notably consumers felt out of touch with the company and where it was going, while at the same time they had high expectations of food companies generally and of Kraft Foods in particular.

The large group events created the backdrop to the second phase of the process, which was an employee purpose and values online community that developed ideas, then refined and filtered them before discussing finally what needed to change to bring the corporate brand to life. To prevent the process becoming too inwardly focused, community members were reminded to think as consumers. Participation was encouraged through a flow of activities, including brainstorms, focus groups and polls and the endorsement of the process by the CEO. The iterative nature of online discussion enabled people to converse their way to ideas and to explore their implications for action. Dozens of themes were developed during ideation in areas such as purpose, positioning and values and then each theme was explored in depth. Ideas were tested against key performance indicators and measured in terms of popularity and importance. The final concepts were explored to ascertain the real meaning and to determine the gap between current reality and aspiration. The resulting brand definition based around 'make today delicious' clearly resonates with employees: several thousand opted to become ambassadors for the brand and participants in the process were twice as likely as non-participants to support the solution. More widely, eight months after the launch, 94 per cent of staff believed the work was worthwhile, 83 per cent believed in what the company was trying to accomplish and 86 per cent knew what they were expected to do to make Kraft Foods successful. As Yeatman argues, co-creation is what smart companies are doing, 'this project is a landmark, involving the collaboration of thousands of employees to co-create the future of an organization. Using co-creation is one of the single most important decisions we have made.'

Creating together with citizens

Etienne Balibar writes of democratization, 'institutions must bring about the conditions for the greatest possible diversification of opinion so that the decisions they produce can effectively be based on the combination of all existing points of view.'[10] Encouraging diversification of opinion sounds admirable as an ideal, but even thinkers with professed strong liberal leanings have not always been so comfortable with its practice.[11] Our social and political arenas talk of democratic intent but perhaps even more than businesses they struggle to embrace sharing knowledge and empowering citizens to co-create their own futures. There is a belief in the primacy of the expertise as embodied in politicians and administrators over the creativity of people, which is perhaps why in many parts of the world there is an alienation from democratic politics. Slawomir Magala, however, is optimistic this will change: 'In communications, especially in hyperlinked societies, meanings can be imported and smuggled and thus the unfinished project of democracy can be retrieved, reinvented, rejuvenated and retried.'[12] In other words, the fluidity of communications can enable the co-creation of public processes.

A good example of this spirit has been Iceland's development of an open approach to the creation of a new constitution.[13] The impact of the financial crisis and the apparent involvement of politicians in it, has created a need for greater transparency and accountability. Consequently citizens have been involved from the start of the process both in face-to-face sessions to set the agenda and then online to discuss and develop ideas. The constitutional council has posted draft clauses and invited comments on the constitution on its website and has used social media to generate interaction. Council meetings are also open to the public and are streamed live on to the website and Facebook. The aim is to create something that is created by and for the people of Iceland. Three caveats ought to be noted. It is much easier to democratize something as specific and concrete as a constitution but much more complex to engage people on an on-going basis with the messy process of governing. The scale and homogeneity of Iceland as an entity makes interaction easier to manage; IBM has more employees than there are Icelanders. It would be much harder to achieve effective participation in a larger country with millions of people and diverse interests. And the number of people that have chosen to engage with the process has been limited, which reminds us of a key principle of this book. Structured participation, whether conducted by governments or businesses, needs the appropriate mechanisms and it has to be nurtured.

As we look to the future, there will be increasing pressure for government and civil institutions everywhere to become more participative if they are to remain relevant. Certainly when people are passionate about a cause, the enabling power of the Internet now empowers citizens to take action where they see fit and increasingly they do. Tuqan (2010) describes how a group of concerned citizens took action after the 2010 Haiti earthquake. As often happens in disasters, many groups and agencies quickly offered help and despatched people. Yet such was the devastation on the ground that there was a lack of coordination and an inability to focus on the most important problems. The solution was a real-time Haiti crisis map, modelled from on-going social media input, web, SMS and email among others. Interestingly, the map was not made by an NGO or government institution, but by a group of students at Tufts University in Massachusetts and volunteers from Ushahidi – an open-source project that was set up to map reports of violence in Kenya in 2008. Tuqan notes, 'the fact that a handful of students could mobilize so quickly to meet such a challenge speaks not only to the power of the individual, but also to the inability of governments to react faster than their citizens to a crisis.'[14]

It seems clear that the desire for people to participate actively in civil society and in some way to define the worlds of which they are part, opens up possibilities for institutions to employ co-creation methods as part of the process of democratization. Even though we put considerable emphasis on our consuming identities, an even more important part of who each of us is, is our identity as a citizen. In this sphere we can both find meaning and sociality; to contribute to a sense of self and to contribute to the world of others. From the institutional perspective there is the real advantage of enhancing relevance for the individuals who connect with and contribute to the way civil society works. This implies a rejection of the Hobbesian view of the dominance of the sovereign power[15] and instead a focus on the individual and their responsibility towards others. As with the commercial organizations we have discussed, the key to this is to bring civil institutions and citizens closer, so that policies become more accountable. This entails the involvement of citizens throughout a process, creating and developing ideas and helping to guide implementation.

Involving citizens in tax compliance

The collection of taxes is not normally one of those areas where people are given an active role. Rather the government determines tax and an agency is then charged with collection. Even if there have been attempts to treat tax-paying citizens as 'customers' there is still a strong feeling of distance between the reluctant tax payer and an impersonal and aloof state (See Figure 8.1). This creates a de-personalized relationship that generates a range of negative attitudes towards the payment of taxes (others get more than me; I pay too much) and the uses to which revenues are put (I don't even drive. Why should I pay for the roads?). This line of thinking combined with a growing sense of individual autonomy encourages people to rationalize why they shouldn't pay the full amount of tax. In the UK, HMRC, which is responsible for the collection of personal taxes and duties, wanted to better understand the way citizens thought about tax and to improve the tax yield by employing a participative approach where solutions could be generated together by management, staff and taxpayers. This was not simply about testing out ideas, but rather trying to get beneath the surface attitudes of people and to encourage them to re-define the process of tax collection and communication. Simply involving people who were conformists would not have been very productive, so there was a deliberate attempt to include people who had cheated on their tax, perhaps because they were rebels or risk takers and liked getting one over on the system. Of the 159 individuals who were involved in interviews, discussions and a large group event, around half had evaded tax at some point. At the outset there was some concern as to how these people could be recruited – and indeed how HMRC managers and staff could talk to them without feeling compromised. Encouraged by the knowledge that their personal details were not to be disclosed and a willingness to express their beliefs, the evaders were more than willing to participate.

The co-creation process, which extended over several months, took away many of the boundaries that existed at the outset between HMRC and citizens. People gave of themselves and HMRC staff responded by demonstrating a willingness to engage and to accept their own failings. As we have observed in other examples, this created a space of safety where people

FIGURE 8.1   An Art from Within drawing that shows the distance between the state and the individual

began to sense problems and solutions independent of their own interests. This included a willingness to work towards a solution that would be detrimental to the philosophies of some of the non-compliant. The core solution that was developed built on the emotional, childlike attitude of many towards paying tax, by creating an approach that focused on shame. This emphasized the reputational risks of non-compliance: 'fateful moments' when we become aware of the unexpected tragic consequences of our actions as our identity and self-esteem is threatened. This emphasis that actions have consequences that affect lives at a personal level taps into the strong individualism that people express when they talk about their relationship to the state while maintaining the authority of the HMRC.

The HMRC example is interesting at many levels. First, it illustrates the importance of managers and staff being open – even to acknowledging the reasons for non-compliant behaviour – to generating the depth of understanding required to become more effective. If staff had simply said they couldn't talk to people who have not paid their taxes, there would have been no possibility of discovery. Second, it shows that the relationship with citizens is a complex one. People can express sometimes very emotional views about a subject, such as tax, yet at another level they can also recognize the rational benefit of tax paying. Getting people to move beyond the superficial requires spending time and building trust. Third, it demonstrates that while a 'customer'-centric view in public services is valuable in defining employee behaviour towards citizens, it is also a metaphor with limits. Staff attitudes, service design and enquiry centres are all vital elements in nurturing a relationship, but there is also a policing role here which in the case of the HMRC involves inspections and fines, emphasizing the need for citizen compliance.

CASE STUDY A Silicon Valley perspective by Y F Juan

'How do you do it in Silicon Valley?' people often ask me.

Silicon Valley can appear to be full of contradictions. Why are people willing to share information with others who are practically strangers? What is the rationale behind the feckless pursuit of new technologies without a known market? How does it sustain innovation that has touched people everywhere in the world over five decades? And most of all, what does the future hold?

Ecosystems

Amongst the many variables of Silicon Valley's ecosystem examined by analysts and scholars, three seem to warrant special attention – ethnic diversity, employment flexibility and clusters.

Ethnic diversity

Fifty per cent of kindergarten students in Mountain View, where Google is headquartered, do not speak English at home.

While ethnic diversity could promote creativity, in practice the causation is not always obvious. Given a critical mass of people with similar ethnic background, an enclave is usually formed and interaction with the mainstream is confined to its fringe. Not a bad thing per se, if you enjoy visiting the old Chinatown in New York City.

Silicon Valley's ethnic communities seem to take the opposite view; despite having the critical mass to build silos, cultural and language affiliations function more as incubators that spin out winning ideas. In other words, founders can nurture a new start-up based on their own blend of competitive advantage instead of requiring MBA handlers from day one. For example, Monte Jade Association with its ethnic Chinese affiliation has been a forum for hardware companies to source hardware design and manufacturing capabilities in Taiwan and China.

Employment flexibility

Look Mom! No employment contract.

California, where Silicon Valley is located, is an 'At-will' state, which is a lawyer's way of saying the employee or employer can break off the employment relationship without liability. At first glance, this may seem to give the employer the upper hand. However, in a knowledge economy, the 'At-will' relationship works both ways. In its battle for talents, Google announced an across-the-board 10 per cent pay increase in January 2011. 'At-will' also allows people to strike out on their own, unencumbered. For instance, founders of two major CRM (Customer Relationship Management) companies, Marc Benioff of Salesforce.com and Tom Siebel of Siebel Systems, were both Oracle alumni.

At the ecosystem level, the seemingly chaotic and fluid flow of talent is not just an ongoing re-jigging of existing capabilities but a manifestation of Schumpeter's creative destruction in inventing new industries. The emergence of Google has created a new field known as SEO/SEM (Search Engine Optimization/Search Engine Marketing) that has grown to US $15+ billion in 2010 in the US alone. Today, Capital One, a financial services company, has a team spending US $100+ million per year on Google related SEO/SEM. Five years ago there was lively debate about whether this task was worth a full time position and ten years ago this function did not exist.

Clusters

Silicon Corridor (Boston), Silicon Alley (New York City), Silicon Forest (Seattle), Silicon Hills (Austin).

A much heralded and imitated feature of Silicon Valley is clusters. Both Michael Porter and Paul Krugman have argued that geographic clusters build competitive firms by intensifying rivalry, fostering specialized suppliers, and creating optimized production networks. Unlike the science parks dedicated to a particular technology in Asia or the 'Silicon X' regions throughout the US, Silicon Valley is unique in its breadth of clusters. From the hardware and communication powerhouses of Intel and Cisco in the South Bay, software leaders like Oracle and Google on the Peninsula, to the new social media/gaming darling of Zynga in San Francisco, the Valley is a super-cluster with a two-hour driving radius. It is hard to imagine that Apple's iPhone and Google's Android –*ceteris paribus* – could have come out of anywhere else except the unique mélange of hardware, software, and creativity that is Silicon Valley.

Having the entire technology stack within a two-hour drive also makes the creation of new companies and industries easier. Instead of asking people to 'think out of the box', the existence of a super-cluster makes the holes between clusters plain to see and the payback for good solutions tangible. Take virtualization, the technical solution that made Cloud Computing mainstream. VMware, the virtualization technology leader, had an eight year head-start on Microsoft when it released its product in 2001. It realized that the physical servers in data centres, ubiquitous in Silicon Valley then, could handle multiple applications at the same time.

Plumbing for the ecosystem

It is one thing to talk about ecosystem structures such as clusters, employment flexibility and diversity, but how are trust and day-to-day information pathways formed? After all, in a place that operates in dog years (seven human years' worth of activities crammed into one), wouldn't people put on blinders and focus on their own silos? The short answer is that Silicon Valley tends to attract those whose natural instinct is to challenge blinders.

There are many ways of connecting organizations and people. At the organization level there are dedicated scouting departments and offices. Honda Motors' Honda Research Institute has a Silicon Valley office that funds new development. Intuit, a $3 billion business and personal finance and tax software company, has an active program to engage external organizations. Industry events such as the Innovation Sandbox, hosted by RSA for the security industry, and company tours organized by Printed Electronics, an eponymous industry event, also connect ideas, people and companies.

For emerging industries, there are venture competitions such as Cleantech Open and Y-Combinator that corral founders, technologists, investors, analysts and reporters in the same room. Professional services companies, such as law firms, regularly host events addressing issues that apply across industries. Stanford University's Product Realization Lab hosts meetings for aspiring students and mentors. Google would not have existed today had its founders agreed to sell their patents to the buyer that Stanford's Office of Technology Licensing had found.

Beyond formal activities there are a myriad of organized but informal gatherings. A cohort of Chief Technology Officers meets monthly to share the latest on Cloud Computing and technology scouting officers regularly swap notes on helping external inventions to take root in internal units. This type of person-to-person sharing provides a safe forum to learn what is new, validate what is working, and get the reality check that may be too sensitive to discuss in the office. Through these personal interactions, bonds are formed and introductions are made that allow new products, companies and industries to emerge, seemingly out of nowhere.

What drives the heightened level of communications and connections, arguably the 'glue' that binds a robust ecosystem with layers of personal and professional relationship, is the need to understand uncertainty and minimize risks for the emerging industries that Silicon Valley is itself creating. If you were leading VMware in the early days, you would have wanted to tell as many people as possible about virtualization to see what resonated. If you are managing Intuit, you want to figure out who to attract into your ecosystem. If you are running Stanford's Office of Technology Licensing, you want to know who should buy what part of your technology portfolio. If you are a founder of a start-up, you want to find out what competing ideas are in the offing. And, if you are a venture investor, you want to know the valuation multiples for the teams and areas that you are interested in.

What lies ahead for silicon valley?

As if the ferocity of competition and the ephemeral half-life of technologies were not enough, a challenge confronting Silicon Valley today is the global competition for ideas, funding and talents. For example, the technology-investing world is buzzing over the recent wave of social buying firms featuring members only, deal-of-the-day/flash sales, and two of the major players have decidedly non-Silicon Valley addresses, GroupOn headquarters in Chicago and Gilt Groupe in New York City. Even Google's venerated advertising supported business model was based on a model pioneered by Overture Services based out of 'low-tech' Los Angeles. Internationally, it was not until the recent introduction of iPhone and Android that Silicon Valley gained a modicum of credibility in mobile devices.

Despite the success of GroupOn and Gilt in the US and the intensifying global competition, I am sanguine about Silicon Valley's pre-eminence as the preferred place to create and nurture new technology companies. If anything, the emergence of the social buying firms is really a testament to Silicon Valley's ability to create technology that integrates into the fabric of everyday life instead of the limited confines of the IT brotherhood. And, truth be told, it just goes to show that technology geeks do not make good shoppers. All the same, the attraction of Silicon Valley is amply demonstrated by the global leader in social media, Facebook. Although it was founded in a dorm room at Harvard University, near Boston's Silicon Corridor, given its novel business model of relying on user generated content, complex technical demand in serving a rapidly growing global user base and its voracious appetite for high quality talents, its move to the heart of Silicon Valley less than a year after its founding is both strategic and, I would argue, inevitable.

Beyond global rivalry, I believe Silicon Valley is embarking on a structural change. This Black Swan event comes from, of all places, the United States Supreme Court. Until its 2010 Bilski v Kappos decision, the conventional wisdom was that only hardware patents could hold up to legal scrutiny. Through the Bilski case the Court signalled that software is largely patentable. The practical implication is to create a new arsenal based on intellectual property that favours larger and older technology firms with both the financial resources to deploy legal counsel and the accumulated patents portfolio as negotiation chips. Kent Walker, Google's General Counsel, indicated as much in his April 2011 blog when Google announced its nearly $1billion bid for Nortel's patent portfolio as a way to maintain its freedom of manoeuvre in developing products and services.

After the Bilski decision it will become more difficult for a start-up to thrive in a space adjacent to an established player, until now a proven way of creating new companies. For example, in the CRM space, it was the creation of Oracle (founded in 1977, revenue $27 billion in 2010) that paved the way for Siebel Systems (founded in 1993, revenue $2 billion in 2005 when it was sold). Similarly, Siebel's efforts in establishing the CRM category made Salesforce.com a successful company (founded in 1999, revenue $2 billion in 2011). If the same space were to be created from scratch today, Oracle could have squashed Siebel before it became an industry leader. Similarly, no investor would fund Salesforce.com's ambition because as soon as it proved its viability with the internet-based delivery method, Oracle and Siebel's lawyers would have blocked its aspirations.

Silicon Valley being what it is, the metamorphosis to compete beyond patentable software and business-process ideas began serendipitously a decade before with Google's multi-sided platform (MSP) business model. Whereas traditional business models are based on the linear value-chain where a company transforms know-how and resources into a product, eg a computer chip, for the buyers, a company using the MSP model marshals its teams and technology to create a platform that enables buyers and sellers to seek out and engage each other. In the case of Google, it collects money from sellers engaged in SEO/SEM because its search technology allows the sellers to target eyeballs with a hitherto unavailable precision and reach, at significantly lower costs. Facebook utilizes a similar framework with two refinements. Eyeballs are collected as users create and consume content without input from Facebook. And Facebook fosters the creation of social apps, such as Zynga's FarmVille, which not only entertains its user base but also generates additional revenue streams. This model is not limited to software/internet solutions. Apple has created a powerful MSP model through the iTune AppStores where vendors around the world create a vibrant ecosystem that Apple alone could not. Better still, taking advantage of consumer device subsidy and contract lock-in as part of the iPhone distribution strategy probably came as an epiphany to most Apple watchers.

As these companies have demonstrated, the ability to effectively execute a winning MSP business model makes it possible for a new entrant to create and dominate a new category that cannot be blocked by patents alone. Of course this does not mean that the ingredients for success of yore – excellence in technology, team and execution are any less vital in actualizing an idea. If anything, the Silicon Valley canine year has just become busier.

Branding with Multi-Sided Platforms (MSP)

The common factor in branding with MSPs is the co-evolution of the product and community ecosystem. While mastery of traditional brand management continues to be important – Apple has not stopped aweing the world since its Super Bowl '1984' TV spot – with MSP-focused branding, managing on-going user experience has become a key lever. For Apple branding extends to being an effective gatekeeper for iPhone Apps so that the user experience is positive and predictable.

Another MSP-focused branding characteristic is the ability to generate and analyze data to test new hypotheses in real-time. According to Andrew Trader, a founder of Zynga, one of the most successful game vendors on Facebook, the company only builds games whose matrices can be measured against its 'reach, retention, and revenue' objectives. Facebook allows Zynga to capture all the usage data in the wild in real-time, a drastic shift in visibility and feedback that was never possible before.

Finally, given the co-evolution of brand with community participation, a unique advantage of MSP branding is that failure need not be a traumatic stigma. Google is known for its product beta launches where users are expected to help inform the direction and continuation of a product. Gmail is probably the most well-known example of a successful beta. Even when betas are unsuccessful, as in the case of Google Wave, which came out with great fanfare in 2009 only to be shut down within 12 months, most people still applaud the company for its technically agility.

'This is how we do it in Silicon Valley,' I said.

It is not for the faint of heart. Silicon Valley is about a diverse group of people who want to make a difference every day. While nobody knows what tomorrow holds, we always wake up looking forward to the challenges ahead.

Y F Juan is an innovation management and commercialization strategist. His blog on related topics, Prometheus Reconsidered, can be found at: **http://prometheusrecon-sidered.blogspot.com**

Conclusion

This chapter has shown that co-creation extends beyond consumers. Indeed we can argue that there is significant potential among other stakeholders because there is an alignment of interests between business partners, employees and citizens and the sponsoring organization. If these groups are part of the sovereign whole it makes sense for them to reach solutions together. Of course this may not always be a comfortable relationship because different parties may value things differently, but as Freeman, Harrison and Wicks note, the primary aspect of corporations is cooperation. They suggest that organizations should be a vehicle 'by which stakeholders are engaged in a joint and cooperative enterprise of creating value for each other.'[16]

Notes

1 Singer, I (2007) *Ingmar Bergman, Cinematic Philosopher: Reflections on His Creativity*, p 5, The MIT Press, Cambridge, Mass

2 'But doth suffer a sea-change, Into something rich and strange.' Ariel in Shakespeare's *The Tempest*

3 Lafley, AG and Charan, R (2008) *The Game-Changer: How You Can Drive Revenue and Profit Growth with Innovation*, p 131, Crown Business, New York

4 Vargo, S L and Lusch, R F (2004) 'Evolving to a New Dominant Logic for Marketing.' *Journal of Marketing* 68, pp 1–17

5 Collins, J and Porras, J (1998) *Built to Last: Successful Habits of Visionary Companies*. Random House Business Books, London

6 Chomsky, Noam (1998) *On Language*, p 171, The New Press, New York

7 Cees van Riel writes of the elite group approach that 'this method measures in the first instance the picture that the managers have of their company, which is not necessarily the same as the view of the company held by other employees or members of target groups.' Van Riel, CBM (1995) *Principles of Corporate Communication*, p 50, Prentice-Hall, Englewood Cliffs

8 Ind, N (2007) *Living the Brand: How to Transform Every Member of Your Organization into a Brand Champion (3rd edition)*, p 76, Kogan Page, London

9 Hemp, P and Stewart, T A (2004) 'Leading Change When Business Is Good: An Interview with Samuel J Palmisano.' *Harvard Business Review* p 65

10 Balibar, E (2008) *Spinoza and Politics*. (Spinoza et la politique, Presses Universitaires de France, 1985.) Trans. Snowdon, P, p121, Verso, London

11 Most notably, JS Mill, who despite his interest in the principle of freedom, was sceptical of democracy. His argument was that people with insufficient education were overly influenced by public opinion and that as a consequence their thinking was done for them. In *On Liberty* (1863) he writes of the 'commonplaces of received opinion' and 'collective mediocrity'.

12 Magala, S (2009) *The Management of Meaning in Organizations*, p 220, Palgrave, Basingstoke, Hants

13 Haroon, S 'Mob rule: Iceland crowdsources its next constitution.' *The Guardian*, 9 June 2011

14 Tuqan, Y (2010) 'If Brands (and Governments) Don't Do Their Job, Someone Else Will Do It for Them.' *Journal of the Medinge Group* 4

15 On the frontispeice of *Leviathan* (1651) the image features a body of the sovereign formed out of the multitude of individuals, who have authorized the sovereign. The inscription reads, 'non est potestas Super Terram qua Comparetur ei' – there is no power on earth that can be compared to him.

16 Freeman, R E, Harrison, J S and Wicks, A C (2007) *Managing for Stakeholders: Survival, Reputation and Success*, p 6, Yale University Press, New Haven, CT

The results

09

- Measuring the benefits of co-creation
  - Measuring the co-creation effect at Danone
- The value of customer closeness
  - Insights from the Brand Together community
- Creating brand value
  - Re-energizing the ebookers brand
- Conclusion

'*Psychologists tend to see creativity exclusively as a mental process [but] creativity is as much a cultural and social as it is a psychological event.*'[1] **MIHALY CSIKSZENTMIHALYI**

In this chapter we will look at the impact of co-creation both directly in terms of the goals set for a process and indirectly in terms of the organizational effect of stakeholder involvement. While the former is easier to measure and helps to justify a particular approach, the latter may be more powerful in that it has the potential to change the way an organization works.

Mihaly Csikszentmihalyi's work on creativity provides an interesting basis for the argument of the wider impact of co-creation. In the Systems Model of creativity he developed, he argued that creative thought and action takes place within a context – what he called a cultural system – that determines how people see problems and how they approach solutions. This provides the framework within which knowledge, values and practices circulate and which determines how individuals create. Whether new ideas are accepted or not is defined by gatekeepers who are also influenced by the cultural system. Gatekeepers are the key conduits through which ideas must flow if they are to be accepted and promoted. When new ideas are adopted they then become absorbed into the culture. There may be some faults within the idea of the Systems Model, not least the overt emphasis on the creative individual – something Csikszentmihalyi spent a lot of time researching – but it does help to overcome the bias of seeing innovation as an esoteric exercise independent of context.

From the co-creation perspective, the Systems Model helps to emphasize the defining role of organizational culture as a context within which innovation occurs. If the culture creates barriers to the flow of knowledge then it also lowers the opportunity for relevant creativity. We can see this in bureaucratic cultures, where the potential for sharing is limited. Burns and Stalker in *The Management of Innovation* argue that bureaucracies are static, internally focused on efficiency, controlling of employees, unresponsive to their environments and generally unpleasant to work in.[2] In contrast, when knowledge is allowed to flow then interesting connections can be made – not least when organizations learn to open themselves up and involve customers and other stakeholders in the process of creation.

One of the core benefits then of co-creation is its ability to liberate knowledge so that people can become more effective contributors. Information about customer behaviour or the attitudes of partners or employee commitment can be released from departmental silos and shared so that people throughout the business can make more powerful contributions.

Another aspect of the Model is the reminder of the power of the gatekeepers. These exist both inside the organization and outside. Inside, these are the key managers who determine whether an innovative idea will be accepted and supported. Externally, these are the important buyers, lead users and media commentators who enjoy significant influence over others. An idea will only become realized if it can negotiate its way through the challenges set by these audiences. Again co-creation is potentially powerful, because it can involve these key gatekeepers in the process. It should be stressed this is not an argument for buying off potential powerful voices of constraint and criticism. Indeed such voices are valuable for killing unsuitable ideas or adjusting ideas in need of change. Rather it helps to ensure, through involvement from an early stage and generally the earlier the better, that gatekeepers contribute their views to the development of the innovation. It would be unfortunate, for example, to design a new piece of sophisticated medical equipment where the number of buyers may be only a few dozen without involving them in the process. The technical output might be good but the product might still fail buyer needs on an important dimension of performance. Similarly, it would be disappointing if an exciting service innovation for a new hospitality experience failed to generate internal commitment, because key managers did not understand, or had not engaged with, the idea. When managers and opinion leaders are involved, ideas are both likely to be more robust and have a stronger likelihood of being realized.

Finally, the Model forces us to recognize the dynamic nature of the process of innovation, for as innovations are selected and implemented they begin to change the cultural system. They set a new direction and establish new templates against which future ideas will be created and evaluated. In co-creation, new knowledge will be absorbed by participants, either directly from the way the organization briefs people, or through people's wider life experience. Reflecting back on the experience of Orange and its use of consumers as ethnographers, we can see that the participants were able to create new ideas because they had absorbed information from the company and also because they could bring their own understanding of how technology could change the way people behave in building and maintaining relationships. Orange's process was successful in that it was clearly a rewarding experience for consumers and opened the eyes of Orange managers as to new possibilities. It also produced some prototyped concepts that could be researched further and evaluated. It is an interesting example of a process where there were some specific results as well as a less tangible sense of cultural change, as managers engaged directly with consumers and learned with them.

The impact of co-creation on culture creates the potential for the development of more customer-centric approaches to innovation. This is something that seems widespread. IBM's *Capitalizing on Complexity*, a study of 1,541 CEOs, found that the expectation was that customers – and in the case of government, citizens – will increasingly demand a better understanding of their needs. Seventy per cent of CEOs said that customers would expect 'new and different services, closely followed by more collaboration and information sharing'. The study noted that improved collaboration has long been a high CEO priority and that in the 2008 report there was a belief that knowing more about customers led to better innovation on their behalf.

Yet there is also a feeling that collaboration is no longer sufficient: 'Today, the watchword is "co-create".'[3]

Measuring the benefits of co-creation

As the belief in the importance of co-creation has grown, so has the feeling that it should be measured. In a study by the London School of Economics (LSE) and Promise titled *Co-creation: New pathways to value*, which reviewed articles from top business, management and social science journals, a range of benefits was suggested.[4] These included direct benefits derived from customer involvement, such as:

- increased speed to market
- lower cost and higher profitability
- better product quality and greater satisfaction
- reduced risk.

The study also noted that there were papers that cited such benefits as enhanced customer satisfaction and commitment, positive word of mouth recommendation and increased attitudinal loyalty. Figure 9.1 suggests the

FIGURE 9.1   Measuring the impact of co-creation

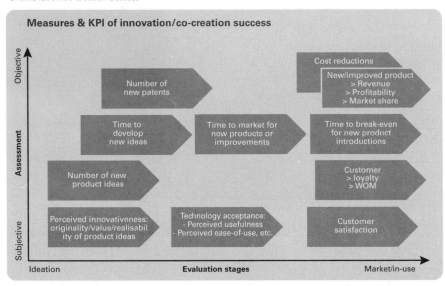

Measuring impact: co-creation KPIs
Product-focused measures and KPIs
of Innovation/Co-creation Success

range of possible impacts. These are charted along an axis from ideation through development to market experience. In the early phase the measures are sometimes subjective, such as perceived innovativeness, but there are also more objective measures of performance based around the time taken to develop new ideas, something several of our interviewees for the book cited as a benefit of more participative processes, and the number of new patents acquired as ideas move beyond ideation to development. Once innovations reach the market there are certain clear points of accountability that become important such as market share and profitability and time to break even for new product introductions as well as measures such as customer satisfaction.

Of course, whether the advocated benefits of co-creation mentioned in the study by the LSE are actually realized will depend in no small part on the way the process is conceived and managed. A co-creation process may generate powerful service innovations that are considered significantly more innovative than those generated by professional service developers[5] or it may produce seemingly unworkable processes such as the customer-generated identity for Gap (see Case Study by Henrik Sjödin above, Chapter 2). For co-creation to produce to its potential a commitment from managers and a sturdy process that involves stakeholders early on and encourages high levels of intra-consumer participation is required, principles we have been arguing in favour of throughout *Brand Together*.

Measuring the co-creation effect at Danone

Danone's brand, Activia, provides a direct insight into the way a co-creation process can deliver direct benefits as well as more indirect ones. Activia is a brand aimed at women with digestive problems which has enjoyed strong growth since its launch. To maintain this and to target communications effectively, Danone built an advisory board of some 400 women. Over five months the online community worked on two distinct projects involving New Product Development (from ideation to implementation) and communications (finding a new positioning for Activia's communications). Community members provided 15,000 contributions and spent 1,300 hours working on the process. It seems clear from the time people were prepared to commit and also from the tone of their conversations that the community generated a strong sense of social connection and meaning-making. One can sense from the online dialogue that the Activia community really substantiates Steve Johnson's point that in large groups connected individuals become smarter. According to an Activia IPSOS study, the community generated 47 per cent more insights than those produced using traditional live methods and the insights were 82 per cent more effective. These insights were overall less polarizing, meaning that they had potential for both existing and potential consumers. Insights generated from the community also led to a new communication campaign resulting in a 9 per cent uplift in base sales (source: Activia Media Study). Ten new product propositions were created, designed and developed and two were approved for launch – the first of which achieved 80 per cent distribution in the first month.

In looking at the key measures and KPIs in Figure 9.1, we can see that the number and quality of ideas generated through co-creation is significant and we can begin to see in this case that the effects of close customer insight begin to feed through into market performance. There is a sense here that the ideas generated have a deep relevance to customer needs and that they are delivered in a tone that is exactly the voice of the consumer – as indeed it was those same consumers that helped create it. Cecile Lux of Danone is of the view that the innovations generated by the community were not that surprising but that their market relevance was strong because of two key factors. First, attention was paid to recruiting individuals who fitted the key market segment. This created a strong shared interest, 'even when we stopped asking them questions they were still discussing the issues'. Second, the quality of the moderation ensured that the right questions were posed at the right time in the right way and that people were then cajoled and supported as the community developed. For Danone the community was an experiment but one that was positively received by managers who learned that it was possible to generate real depth and specific insights from such a process.

The value of customer closeness

Many organizations express the desire to be close to their customers and other stakeholders and they develop strategies and tools to achieve this. In particular, social media affords an opportunity for organizations to become part of their customers' worlds. As we saw with *more!*, however, that also creates a responsibility for employees to be actively engaged in responding to comments and requests. Closeness is highly valued but it carries with it the obligation to listen and respond continuously. This generates pressure inside the organization in terms of the willingness to allocate resources to an ongoing dialogue and it creates the challenge of knowing what to listen to. The more successful an organization is in listening to its customers, the harder it is to do. IBM's study reinforces this: CEOs increasingly recognize the importance of making effective and rapid decisions, but they also feel 'overwhelmed by data while still being short on insight'.[6] There is a need therefore for better analysis and the creation of relevant knowledge that can reduce the feeling of uncertainty and produce better answers. This points us to the important role of mediating customer closeness. It is possible to become so entwined with customers and their lives that drawing out the relevant strands of thought becomes difficult. Mediators of conversations, whether inside or outside the organization or indeed a combination of the two, need to understand the goals and strategies and the innovation trajectory of the business, but they also need to be connected into the wider world so that they understand the future opportunities that may emerge and that may be relevant as they mediate and interpret.

No matter how the analysis and coding of content is done in identifying concepts and properties, the mediator will introduce bias that gives weight to some points over others. This may mean a theme is under or overrepresented but if the content is to create the potential for action then this interpretative process is vital. The requirement for faster decisions means we have to be selective and focus on those things that seem to matter most. Régis Debray points out that people communicate all the time but that there is a difference between the transitory conversations that we have – the content of which is mostly forgotten – and what he calls 'transmission', the key ideas and phrases that are remembered and have a cultural impact that goes beyond the immediate.[7] As Gagliardi writes, 'actions, like thoughts and speeches, are contingent signs, destined to vanish if they are not reified.'[8] This might seem worrying but it is inevitable – the writer Borges wrote a very powerful short story about the need we have to ignore and forget what goes on around us.[9]

Managers clearly have a strong motivation to get closer to customers both to generate relevant innovations that align with the brand and to reduce risk. While social media is a tool that can help with this, the benefit of tailored communities and events is dominant in two areas. First, with a closed community it is possible to get close to the sort of consumers that align with business strategy. For example, if the aim is to generate a product targeted at non-customers from a new age and geographic segment, specifically these people can be recruited. This sort of selectivity is far harder to achieve through open communities. Second, while good facilitation and analysis is vital in selecting the most important ideas and concepts, communities and events enable managers to be direct participants. So while managers receive reports and presentations on the outputs, they are also able to layer their own personal experience of having been part of a mixed customer/company group that has spent two days together working on first name terms, drawing pictures, brainstorming ideas and constructing prototypes. This both adds a rich personalized experience to the reading of the report and enables managers to be more engaged and questioning during discussion of the results. We might add a word of caution here, in that a manager's singular experience can also colour the reading of the outputs or lead to the formation of an abstract idea that fails to take into account the experiences of other groups in the process.

Insights from the Brand Together community

We can argue that customer closeness benefits both the company and the individual. The company generates above average returns and enhances its brand value as a result of being relevantly innovative and the individual receives the opportunity to buy and use new products and services. But we should also emphasize the co-creation experience of community participants. Does being part of a community make people feel close to an organization? Do they feel they are being listened to? Do they think their contributions are appreciated?

One interesting result of brand owners' attempts to connect to customers is that past endeavours seem to have had a limited impact. Participants largely perceive brands to be artificial and distant. The positive aspect though is that they are open to the notion of engaging with brands as long as brand owners are 'listening' and 'showing a genuine interest' (See Figure 9.2).

The tone of the comments demonstrates that people do not expect an instrumental attitude from companies but rather a sense of participation on equal terms that is both reciprocal and personal.

> They would be telling me about ideas in the pipeline and how they develop them behind the scenes

> On the whole I would rather they listened to me rather than just talked at me

> We would have a discussion about current products, how it could be improved and they would be mostly interested in me

> They would be asking me what I want in a product

The potential of companies to conduct this sort of dialogue, as we observed earlier, is much to do with the attitude they adopt towards people; whether

FIGURE 9.2   What would you like a brand to be asking you?

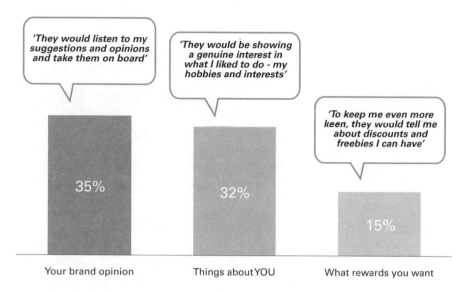

What would you like a brand to be asking you?
(n=173)

'They would listen to my suggestions and opinions and take them on board'

'They would be showing a genuine interest in what I liked to do - my hobbies and interests'

'To keep me even more keen, they would tell me about discounts and freebies I can have'

35%   32%   15%

Your brand opinion   Things about YOU   What rewards you want

they see consumers as objects or as stakeholders involved in the joint production of value. Yet it is also to do with the mechanisms, and the question here is whether online communities are a good place to hold these conversations. Almost everyone who has taken part in communities (n=210) feels that they can share their honest views and opinions and 70 per cent feel that it allows them to be more creative. Additionally 63 per cent believe that their contributions have a significant impact, which suggests most see it as a good way of interacting, although there is perhaps an opportunity here to improve demonstrable evidence of the impact of community generated ideas. In Figure 9.3 we can also see that people who participate in communities develop a greater empathy with brands.

Engaging in a dialogue reduces the distance people feel towards a brand, because instead of one-way communication where people are being told about things, there is a sense here of the to and fro negotiation of meaning that makes us feel part of the subjects being discussed. This helps to make people more loyal towards the brand and potential advocates for it.

It's always good to have a bit of member loyalty, like the brand loyalty people can feel from being part of the process

If you worked with me, or read my blog or Facebook, you would hear about my favourite brand all the time

FIGURE 9.3 Up close and personal

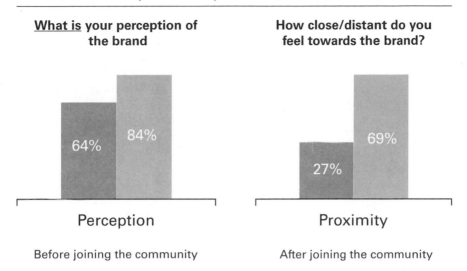

What is your perception of the brand	How close/distant do you feel towards the brand?
64% 84%	27% 69%
Perception	Proximity

Before joining the community   After joining the community

Creating brand value

This book is called *Brand Together: how co-creation generates innovation and re-energizes brands*, because we want to emphasize the framework of the brand as an ever-present element in co-creation. We recognize that not all the companies we have interviewed talk in terms of the brand – although interestingly the Brand Together community members do even though they sometimes reject the jargon of co-creation. Yet even when managers don't mention the terminology of branding, it is still there in the background determining the processes and helping to focus the outputs. Organizational statements about brand visions and values may sometimes look like window dressing but they are normally built on the roots and aspirations of the business and therefore contain a truth that people can engage with. So even if innovators and engineers are not explicitly aware of the meaning of a brand vision or value, they are still using the ideas implicitly as they design software programs or in-car systems.

For example, the way a BMW is designed and engineered is different from a Lexus or a Mercedes because of the long held and carefully nurtured set of principles that determines how staff see the car and the delivery of the driver experience. Adopt a narrow definition of brand and you won't see product engineering as part of it, but if you see the brand as something the customer experiences through both tangible and intangible elements, then how a car drives, the performance of the engine, the braking system, the aerodynamics, all matter. They help to define what is distinct about a BMW. It also serves to remind us that one of the benefits of brand-inspired innovation is that it helps to create a sense of authenticity; a feeling that BMW designed and produced this car and somehow no one else could. Authenticity creates credibility for the brand and delivers customer appeal because it expresses a sense of individual identity. Yet we should also understand that authenticity is not fixed but always changing as the brand evolves and consumers buy other products and take part in different experiences.[10]

The designer Peter Saville once noted, 'the best brands are constantly morphing packages.'[11] How they morph comprises evolution of the product or service itself and the positioning and presentation of the brand. These aspects are clearly linked because a change in one area of product performance will impact on how the brand is positioned while a change in positioning will define how a consumer perceives performance.

As we saw in the case of Barclays and its student account, one of the virtues of co-creation is the capacity for helping to define the content of the product and the way it should be positioned in the market. Innovation-led approaches to co-creation tend to ignore or underplay the latter. Coming from a brand perspective we would argue that both are important because consumers do not buy just a product or a service but rather an experience. The implication is that the whole brand is important. To extend our BMW example, how consumers experience ownership and driving the car is to do with the technical performance but it is also to do with every point of customer contact including styling, advertising, graphics, online, showrooms, people and after sales service. Brands that can offer a unique, consistent and superior experience can build emotional commitment that generates greater levels of brand loyalty and even evangelism.[12]

The value of this is that it helps to build brand equity – the positive association people have towards a brand that determines their willingness to start or continue a relationship with it. Equity can be measured using such metrics as awareness, relevance, perceived quality and loyalty. It is also possible to extend equity measurements into determining the financial value of a brand by looking at the net present value of discounted cash flows that can be attributed to it. The importance of innovation in this context should not be underestimated. As markets change and the equity of a brand shifts, organizations need to be forever improving existing revenue streams and searching for new ones.

Re-energizing the ebookers brand

The online travel booking service, ebookers, which operates in 13 European markets, provides an appropriate example of how a brand can go through a process of change while maintaining unity of customer experience around a key positioning idea. ebookers had grown through the acquisition of several online operations and had melded them together, but to seize the benefits of commercial and marketing economies the company wanted to harmonize itself around a common product range, service offer, communications approach and look and feel. Given the highly competitive nature of online travel, there was a strong feeling that this process ought to be steered by a real insight into customer attitudes and behaviour. Yet, one consequence of the way the company had developed was an almost complete lack of hard information or insight about its customers. Who were they? What was going on in their lives? What were they looking for? How could ebookers be more appealing to them?

The co-creation programme that ebookers embarked on, which combined small group discussions and a large workshop, was designed to generate insights into people's needs and to co-create a positioning together with staff of what their ideal ebookers would be like. The process provided valuable and surprising insights into points of continuity and also difference across Europe. A point of consistency is the attitude of people towards travel. Nowadays individuals increasingly define themselves by their holidays and the experiences they have. It has become a topic of conversation at social gatherings, a feature of online discussion and recommendation and a source of identification. A point of difference is the confidence towards travel and particularly online booking. At one end of the spectrum are mature online travel markets like the UK and Finland. At the other, are markets displaying lower confidence, most notably France. Also country attitudes show clear differences when it comes to rational components of choice (such as price) versus emotional components (such as anxiety). The British are particularly hungry for more and new experiences while the Swiss and Germans are full of anxiety about quality.

Using the insights from the workshop and a quantitative analysis based on value mapping – those elements that are most important in brand choice – ease of use emerged as an important element. This led to a co-created positioning idea around making the experience of booking as easy as possible. This made sense for staff because it was already a key element that had been built into the brand and was clearly deliverable, and it made sense for consumers, especially in more mature markets. As consumers become more confident they look to multiple sources to gain information, they don't need ebookers to excite them and they don't rely on ebookers as an arbiter of quality. But they do want the experience of booking to be quick, intuitive and trouble-free.

Armed with these insights and with a clear sense of what the ebookers brand needed to focus on to be successful, a brand roadmap was created to generate brand preference by linking corporate strategy, brand strategy and the customer journey (See Figure 9.4). The clarity of the map was vital in an organization where lots of people come from a technology background and are sceptical about branding.

The result of the co-creation process steered an overall brand positioning across Europe that determined everything from product selection to page design to personnel development. It both reinforced the things that were already important for the brand and provided a template for ongoing innovation.

Following the launch, there were eight consecutive quarters of revenue growth in excess of 20 per cent measured by value of gross bookings,

FIGURE 9.4 Linking business strategy to brand preference

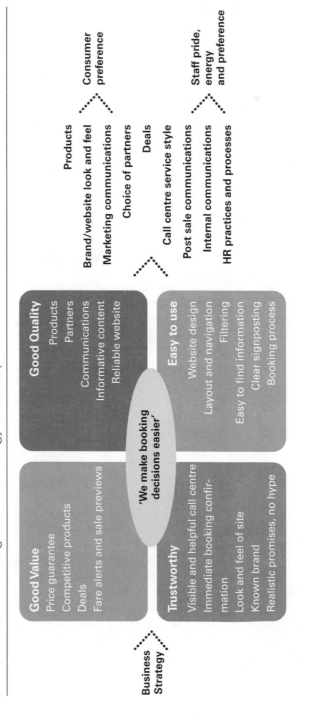

Business Strategy

'We make booking decisions easier'

Good Value
Price guarantee
Competitive products
Deals
Fare alerts and sale previews

Good Quality
Products
Partners
Communications
Informative content
Reliable website

Trustworthy
Visible and helpful call centre
Immediate booking confirmation
Look and feel of site
Known brand
Realistic promises, no hype

Easy to use
Website design
Layout and navigation
Filtering
Easy to find information
Clear signposting
Booking process

Products
Brand/website look and feel
Marketing communications
Choice of partners
Deals

Consumer preference

Call centre service style
Post sale communications
Internal communications
HR practices and processes

Staff pride, energy and preference

significantly outstripping the growth of most competitors. Before the process spontaneous brand awareness was 8 per cent. Six months later, awareness had risen to 18 per cent. Prompted awareness was 70 per cent pre-launch and then stabilized at 82 per cent with virtually no ongoing advertising support. Year on year growth of traffic from sources that ebookers attribute to branding (customers searching specifically for the ebookers name) was up 47 per cent year on year. Conversion on brand name pay per click was four times that of conversion on normal pay per click. Twelve per cent of total traffic now comes from people who type ebookers.com directly into Google/browser bar. Prior to launch the figure was 5 per cent.

Conclusion

In this chapter we have argued that innovation must be seen within the context of a system. A company can have an exemplary process in terms of discovery, ideation, development and filtering but still fail to be an effective innovator because the outputs fail to see the light of day. Leaders and managers are vital gatekeepers who can help to ensure that good ideas make their way to the market, or they can be guilty of inertia, too concerned with meeting this quarter's figures or dealing with on-going problems to give sufficient emphasis to innovation. When organizational insiders are supportive then co-creation can yield strong results because it already includes the customer perspective. This may not always be right of course and co-creation is really too young to generalize whether it has a better record of innovation than more closed models, but it should help to get things to market quicker, while reducing risk. In particular, we sense from our research that co-creation is particularly adept at getting to an effective voice for communications. However, we would not wish to over-egg this point relative to the substance of generating content innovation. Co-creation can clearly help to design and implement products and services so that the brand as experienced by the customer is relevant and appealing. It is the potential of co-creation to address both the tangible and intangible attributes of the brand that make it so interesting.

Notes

1 Csikszentmihalyi, M (1999) 'A Systems Perspective on Creativity' in *Creative Management and Development (3rd edition),* ed Henry, J, p 3, Sage Publications, London

2 Burns, T and Stalker, G M (1994) *The Management of Innovation.* Oxford University Press, New York

3 *IBM: Capitalizing on Complexity.* Research based on 1,541 face-to-face interviews with CEOs worldwide between September 2009 and January 2010, p 41

4 LSE Enterprise and Promise (2009) *Co-creation: new pathways to value*

5 Matthing, J, Sandén, B and Edvardsson, B (2004) 'New service development learning from and with customers.' *International Journal of Service Industry Management,* 15(5), pp 479–98

6 *IBM: Capitalizing on Complexity* (See note 3, above) p 28

7 Debray, R (2000) *Transmitting Culture.* (Transmettre, 1997, Editions Odile Jacob.) Trans. Rauth, E, Columbia University Press, New York

8 Gagliardi, P (2006) 'Exploring the Aesthetic Side of Organizational Life' in *The Sage Handbook of Organization Studies,* eds Clegg, S, Hardy, C, Lawrence, T and Nord, W, p 570, Sage, Thousand Oaks, California

9 Borges makes this point in his short story, '*Funes, His Memory*' (1944), where a boy called Ireneo Funes has a riding accident that leaves him able to observe everything in great detail and to remember it all. Borges' narrator says that he suspects that Funes is not good at thinking: 'to think is to ignore (or forget) differences, to generalize, to abstract.' Funes also finds it hard to operate in daily life because he is virtually incapable of 'general, platonic ideas'.

10 Petersen, R A (2005) 'In search of authenticity.' *Journal of Management Studies,* 42(5), pp 1083–98

11 Interview at Belgrade design and branding week, May 2006

12 Iglesias, O, Singh, J J and Batista-Foguet, J M (2011) 'The role of brand experience and *affective commitment* in determining brand loyalty.' *Journal* of *Brand Management,* 18(8), pp 570–82

Five key questions

- What's co-creation for?
- Who is involved?
- How to manage?
- How to reward?
- What are the limitations of co-creation?
- And finally

'*Those who never dare to break the rules never surpass them.*' BERNINI

Co-creation in its currently practised form is in its infancy which suggests there is still plenty of growing to do. Co-creation will evolve and change along with technology and people's changing attitudes towards participation. In this chapter we will look at some of the key defining themes of co-creation that reflect where it has got to and where it might go in the future (also see below Doron Meyassed's case study on 'What does the future of co-creation look like?'). Here we will pose five questions that build on the core themes in *Brand Together*. Any organization thinking about embarking upon or extending its approach to co-creation ought to consider how it might answer these questions as they are designed to encourage managers to pause and reflect. Similarly amidst all the interest in and euphoria about co-creation and its potential, we will also indicate where dangers might lurk.

What's co-creation for?

Organizations understand the vital importance of innovation. Chief Executives talk about it, managers nurture it and consumers expect it. Yet it is also a potentially disruptive process that interferes with well-laid plans and day-to-day operations. And innovation has historically suffered from high failure rates which add to the challenge. Consequently innovators find that generating new ideas and products is at the same time exciting and laden with anxiety. To help reduce anxiety and improve the chances of success, organizations need to get close to consumers. Enabled by, although not dependent on, technology co-creation provides the opportunity not only to ask consumers their opinions, but also to engage them fully in the process of conceiving, designing and developing new products and services.

Co-creation, as we have defined it, is of course not the only way of reaching a high level of connectivity but it has two important virtues. First, it creates the possibility of recruiting the right individuals to participate, where 'right' means those who best match the innovation goals of the business. This is different from other forms of open innovation where anyone can contribute. Second, it can involve people in exploring beneath the surface of their lives to get to the real issues they face. Here time is the key factor because the nature of large-scale workshops lasting two days and continuous communities provides the opportunity for depth. For example, Virgin Media consumers spend an average of 10 minutes 59 seconds per visit – twice as much as they do on Facebook. This depth is valuable not only in helping to establish the tangible aspects of the innovation but also in defining the appropriate language and imagery when it comes to the marketing process.

As to what people do in co-creation, this is determined by the innovation focus. As we have seen with some examples, such as Barclays and students or HMRC and tax-payers, there is a very clear purpose to co-creation. It is designed to help solve a dilemma with a specific audience through involvement. The other type of co-creation is less purposive and more informative as an organization and its customers explore on an ongoing basis the innovation possibilities. In both cases we should remember that the lens of the brand and what it means for people will steer participants and the ideas they develop, and form the basis of managerial judgements. The potential for co-creation then is to reduce innovation risk by involving those consumers who may buy and use the co-created outputs.

Who is involved?

When talking about co-creation the temptation is to immediately reference consumers, but we should remind ourselves that co-creation is broader than that and can be used as a process to involve business partners, employees, citizens and indeed any other stakeholder group. The practicalities of involvement may change when talking to different stakeholders but the philosophy remains the same – that everyone can be creative if conditions are supportive. This thought can jar with some because we tend to put creativity on a pedestal. Certain artists, musicians, writers and architects seem to be possessed of visionary ideas that the rest of us cannot emulate. Yet we would argue that if you create the right environment, nurture people and establish a bond of trust, then individuals become smarter and the group becomes more creative. When people are enabled to bring their whole selves to co-creation, they also bring their diverse world experiences and skills, which in turn create interesting and surprising connections. This points to the importance of the collective group or community as an entity in its own right. One of our key arguments has been that even if a community is designed to deliver a specific output, it should not be instrumentalized. Managers must see co-creation as a coming together of diverse stakeholders to create something valuable for all. So rather than adopting the perspective of the organization, managers should pay attention to the space they create together with participants where ideas are exchanged, learning takes place and meaning is found.

How to manage?

If managers think of co-creation as a joint exercise of value creation that is determined together with others, it suggests a set of managerial attitudes that involve such soft skills as listening, empathizing and demonstrating humility. As we saw in the Brand Together community, the strongest area of complaint is a lack of attentiveness from the facilitator/organization. People are willing to give of their time because they believe their ideas have meaning and they are being listened to. If ideas fail to get an adequate response or there is poor feedback, disillusionment rapidly sets in. One vital tip here for managers is that co-creation creates a responsibility; it requires the organization to understand that the ideas developed by the community are psychologically owned by the community. Whatever happens to the ideas, people need to be treated as insiders and to feel that they are valued participants.

In terms of managing large-scale groups and communities, we would stress three vital aspects. First, the right question needs to be posed – something that is relevant for the organization and inspiring for participants. This requires time to be spent at the front end of the process evaluating what is already known and what needs to be unlocked. This requires managers to challenge themselves and to be critical of the way things may have been done in the past; something that can be uncomfortable when it confronts deeply held beliefs. Second, managers need to approach co-creation with an open mind. Within the framework of the overarching question there has to be an allowance for the unexpected. Approach a community with the attitude that you already know the answer and you are unlikely to generate new, un-thought-of possibilities that may take the brand in surprising yet rewarding directions. Third, attention must be paid to the mediation process. Co-creativity does not just happen. It requires directing and nurturing. Problems have to be dealt with as they occur and people's needs have to be addressed. And at the end, time needs to be spent synthesizing the outputs and generating actionable ideas.

The exact requirements of co-creation management will depend of course on how it is used. Sometimes organizations use it for certain stages of the innovation process, such as idea generation or development or filtering. As these are more self-contained they generate input as an alternative to other forms of research. However, what seems to be emerging are organizations that embrace co-creation as a philosophy such that consumers and other stakeholders are involved from early stage ethnography through ideation to commercialization. This is more robust as a method because it ensures that ideas do not fall down or get compromised in stage gaps. At the same time it does generate a lot of content. For example, the Brand Together community, which ran for only 52 days, generated 14,130 contributions from 236 members who collectively spent 1,935 hours online. This material has to be processed and key messages drawn out. The implication is that taking co-creation seriously requires resources and an on-going commitment.

At this stage in the co-creation life cycle the upside of the task for managers involved with co-creation is that there seems to be a strong interest inside organizations. The people we interviewed for *Brand Together* consistently reported that their colleagues were intrigued by the opportunity of co-creation and were more than willing to participate. Part of the value of this is that it helps to make innovation an integral part of the organization. Maarten Korz of Rabobank argues that one of the virtues of creating innovation networks within the organization and sharing innovation practices widely through participation is that it sparks new ideas everywhere. Innovation then ceases to be a silo activity and becomes a way of life. With widespread involvement, both the quantity and the quality of ideas improves and the potential for action increases. The Nobel prize winner Linus Pauling once noted that the way to get a good idea was to have lots of ideas. Not only is co-creation ideal for producing lots of ideas but it is also powerful for making sure the good idea sees the light of day.

How to reward?

It seems clear that the dominant motivation for people to take part in participative processes such as co-creation, is intrinsic. They give their time and their intellect because of the benefit it generates for them as individuals in terms of learning and meaning-making and it is also a socializing activity that is enjoyable for the potential of sharing. Extrinsic incentives are a secondary feature in that they help people to rationalize their participation. This emphasis on intrinsics versus extrinsics comes through clearly from previous research among employees and also is supported by the evidence of the Brand Together community. As suggested by Frederick Herzberg, the difference is that you can only create satisfaction through intrinsic factors, but you can create dissatisfaction by failing to pay sufficient attention to extrinsics.[1] Therefore, managers must give due weight to the effect of extrinsic factors, otherwise dissatisfaction may emerge, as this comment from the Brand Together community suggests:

> Dear Prof Ind – I like your style! I wish I'd thought of your idea. Co-creation is a great money-spinning concept [. . .] because you can pay 300 people a few quid for coming up with ideas, developing them and showing which ones they like. The company gets good ideas cheaply that they can then implement without as much costly R&D, you get to write a book on it and we get a few quid and a sense of yay I helped think of that when the ideas are acted on. Genius!!!

The inference here is twofold. First, co-creation practitioners need to be attentive to the possibility that in future participants will demand more from the organization. Second, practitioners need to listen to participants to ensure that their intrinsic needs are being met. This may become increasingly important if co-creation fatigue begins to emerge. Attention may then need to be paid to more inventive methods and perhaps greater use of game genres to re-energize co-creation itself.

What are the limitations of co-creation?

Co-creation is a process that, when well-managed, can be enormously effective – as many of the cases in this book have shown. However, it does have some dangers and limitations:

1 A particular area of concern is connected to opening up the organization. To make the most of co-creation the organization needs to treat customers and other stakeholders as insiders. This suggests a degree of transparency and openness which may feel threatening. Some protection is afforded to companies by asking people to sign non-disclosure agreements but the widespread involvement of several hundred people discussing and creating together increases the possibility that innovation strategies and new product ideas are leaked. The balance of how much to share and what to hold back has to be determined on a case by case basis but we would always urge organizations to be as open as they can be. As a generalization we might say that it becomes ever harder to operate behind closed doors, partly because the online world of gossip and rumour means people get to know corporate intentions, and partly because complexity means organizations increasingly have to share knowledge with others as part of the process of innovation.

2 Connected to the whole issue of openness and disclosure is the thorny subject of intellectual property. In the current model, the ideas that are created through co-creation are generally the property of the sponsoring organization. Until now this model has been accepted because of the intrinsic rewards of participation. But the case of a class action in 2011 by the bloggers who had helped deliver the

online Huffington Post may suggest a different attitude in the future. The bloggers were seemingly happy providing their services for free, until Arianna Huffington sold the Post to AOL for $315 million. This sparked the dissatisfaction mentioned in the previous section, changing some of the bloggers from willing participants into plaintiffs. One of the ways that co-creation may develop in response to this is to do as Doron Meyassed notes in the case study below and to develop a different approach to intellectual property, where participants do have a share in the outcomes.

3 Many of the cases in this book are of a non-technical nature (yoghurts, telecom services, bank accounts), but can co-creation work in more technical arenas? There might be some scepticism that this requires too much knowledge, but we see that co-creation techniques have been successfully used in the design and development of cars, motorbikes, airplane interiors and IT services. As long as the orientation of co-creation is towards developing products and services that consumers use, there should not be a category limit, although lengthy time scales may make it complex. When innovation becomes oriented towards business buyers, the co-creators cease being consumers and start being business partners. Overall we would argue that co-creation is potentially relevant in all spheres – the only limitation is a managerial willingness to break out of self-imposed business models and practices.

CASE STUDY   Doron Meyassed provides an insight into the trends that are driving co-creation

What does the future of co-creation look like?

Any attempt to predict the future is problematic. This is especially true with a practice that is increasingly enabled by technology change. So I'd like to offer a set of hypotheses and thoughts about what the future of co-creation may look like. These are all based on solid thinking, experience and a thorough analysis of trends. They have emerged from a team-wide debate and panel session and the experience of running and analysing large-scale co-creation programmes. We have also interviewed dozens of CMOs, CIOs and Insight Directors as to where the future of co-creation lies. And most importantly, we are constantly monitoring technological trends and investing heavily in developing our own collaboration tools and technologies.

So here are nine ideas on the future of co-creation:

1 Co-creation becomes 100 times as powerful: The most common thought that crosses our mind on a day-to-day basis is 'we haven't even begun to scratch the surface of what co-creation can do'. Technological, societal and business trends all reaffirm

this point of view. Technological advances will allow us to collaborate more visually and far more quickly. Automated translation technology will allow us to collaborate globally in our mother tongues. And mobile technology will open new avenues for insight as we become able to overlay what 'people say' with what they do. But technology isn't the only thing that will make co-creation more effective. Perhaps far more important is the developing scientific understanding of how to get large groups to collaborate effectively. A huge amount is being invested, devising new models, tools and techniques to improve the effectiveness of collaboration. Finally, there is increasing evidence that the world's population is getting more and more interested and motivated to participate in co-creative endeavours. Which brings us to our next point. . .

2 Participants start to care as if it were their own business: The most important determinant of a successful co-creative endeavour is how much its participants care. But it isn't easy to get consumers to care about inventing a new drink (often a detailed process) or a communication campaign for a financial product (which may appear a dry challenge). Getting people to care costs time and money. But businesses are increasingly willing to invest in motivating people. They are making bold moves including issuing their consumer co-creators with shares in their businesses. Furthermore, co-creation practitioners are becoming particularly good at using psychology to motivate and unite large groups of collaborators. And as a general societal trend, we are increasingly seeing people define their status by what they share rather than by what they own.

3 Co-creation gets used for more problems, earlier on in the process. Co-creation is already being directed at an increasing number of challenges. As the practice continues to improve we would expect its rate of growth to be exponential. But far more interesting is the fact that co-creation is being brought in earlier and earlier in the problem solving process. Organizations tend to have an implicit view of problem-solving. Experts generate ideas and thinking, the 'layman' tests and validates them. This is a difficult mindset to change and will take time. But we are increasingly seeing organizations open up to the idea of involving people from day one, helping to scope the problem in the first place and devise the strategies and innovations to solve it. An increasing level of evidence affirms the view that doing so generates superior innovations and strategies.

4 Co-creation will also exist in a disintermediated form: Bankers and traders wouldn't dream of making decisions without their Bloomberg terminal. It provides them with real time, tailored data that helps make dozens of daily well-informed decisions. The kinds of decisions a brand or marketing manager needs to make on a daily basis are no different; dozens of them about promotions, pricing, packaging, advertising and distribution. So what is the marketing world's equivalent of the Bloomberg terminal? In the future we will see individuals within organizations interacting directly with their community of consumer co-creators to help make dozens of daily, real-time decisions. This is a fundamental shift from today, where all co-creation endeavours are managed and facilitated by a central group of people.

5 Co-creation will be seen as the most powerful way of being consumer-centric: I can't remember the last time I read an annual report that didn't have 'consumer

centricity' as a core pillar of the strategy. But being genuinely consumer-centric is tough, expensive and often slow. You simply can't get consumers to input into all parts of the business in an informed way. It takes time to educate and develop them. But recent examples of co-creation communities, such as those run by Pepsico, Danone, Orange and Virgin Media, show how collaborative tools can make genuine consumer centricity affordable and possible. These organizations work with pools of several hundred consumers who know the brand inside out. People can give feedback from their mobiles and laptops, without having to leave home. And they can do so 20 times a day while only spending 30 minutes on the task.

6   Brands learn to trust co-creators. In a recent co-creative endeavour, Diageo invited 200 consumers to help them develop a brand strategy for one of their brands. At the end of the process, Diageo then invited the community of co-creators to choose the ad agency for the brand, after sharing with them the different pitches! Have you ever heard of an organization that believed in the power of its consumers so much that they let them influence their choice of ad agency? Diageo experienced the power of co-creation. As brands start to trust the consumer more as a problem-solving partner, they are empowering them to contribute in ever more influential ways. Expect to see brands releasing raw financial data to let consumers and stakeholders crunch it and try to find improvements. Expect to see co-creative projects releasing business model information, logistical challenges and budgetary constraints. And with this greater trust, expect to see more effective co-creation.

7   A co-creative mishap: As brands open up and invite more people inside, I would imagine we will see one or two high profile errors or mistakes like a competitor infiltrating the process or an innovation being leaked. As more and more players enter the market it is possible that some will not take the needed precautions to protect intellectual property (IP) and reputation. If a co-creative mishap does occur, it is sure to tighten the industry, bringing in better checks and measures to ensure confidentiality and IP protection.

8   It will liberate the experts: While collaborative principles of innovation and development have been around a long time, they have always been overshadowed by the idea of the individual breakthrough. From Albert Einstein to Steve Jobs we tend to look for heroes and saviours. We develop unrealistic pressures and expectations that the experts will generate the answer. I genuinely hope that the growth in co-creation will liberate the expert. Experts will feel less of the pressure to be the hero inventor and more freedom to collaborate with others. A reduction in pressure and a more open mindset will drive creativity. It will undoubtedly make the working life of an expert a more interesting, fulfilling and enriching experience.

9   It will empower the 'layman': I may consider myself an expert in brand, marketing and innovation, but I am pretty much a layman in everything else that exists in our universe. The more we work in co-creation, the more we are reminded of the sheer power of the 'layman'. The best ideas emerge from them. And they bring in concepts, ideas and theories from diverse fields which provide new perspectives. My personal hope is that the experience of partaking in co-creation will empower us. As laymen we will realize our immense value to any problem-solving exercise, even in subjects we know little or

nothing about. A more empowered population that feels confident in its ability to help and influence the solving of any problem is perhaps the most exiting prediction of all.

We can't help but paint a positive picture of the future. The more we interact with co-creation, the more our views are reaffirmed. The mega-trends support our point of view; organizations are becoming more global, speed of innovation is ever more important, consumers are interested in using their free time to input into productive endeavours and technology is opening new possibilities. While some of our predictions may not come true, we feel confident about one thing; co-creation is going to revolutionize the way humans solve problems.

Doron Meyassed is Director and Founder of Promise Communities

And finally

Throughout this book the ideas generated by the Brand Together community have permeated our arguments. This has lent weight to our ideas not only about the way co-creation is practised but by what it might become in the future. In particular the community wholeheartedly took up the challenge of innovating co-creation that was detailed at the end of Chapter 6. It is very difficult to capture the richness of the ideas and discussions that were developed. Nevertheless we will conclude *Brand Together* with an insight into the process and the results. The former is interesting because it illustrates the two-way flow between community members and facilitators, while the latter is instructive because it shows the creativity, commitment and community spirit of the participants.

The Innovation Challenge started with a detailed invitation to community members to help invent the future of co-creation. This generated a diverse range of ideas which were then ranked, sorted and grouped by the facilitators. The broad themes were then given back to the community members and they were invited to form teams around the topics they thought were most interesting and impactful. Members then submitted their own detailed suggestions to the team for discussion. To give some structure to this stage, members had to answer some specific questions and were invited to sketch out their idea with visuals where appropriate:

- your name
- your idea
- the problem you are trying to solve
- how would it work?
- why would people bother taking part?
- what would your idea look like?

FIGURE 10.1   Community member suggestion: skype it all over

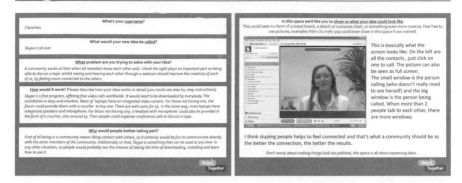

Once the suggestions had been made the facilitators again ranked and sorted the ideas into a final eight propositions which were then discussed and filtered by community members into the things they most wanted to see implemented. This toing and froing was key. While the facilitators created focus, the community members were able to explore different possibilities and retain their sense of ownership of the ideas.

The themes that emerged as important to community members reinforce many of the ideas featured in the book. Members want organizations to be participative and provide prompt and adequate feedback, and they suggest mechanisms for doing this. They also argue for techniques to help build trust among members. They would like to see greater opportunities for self-selecting teams that want to tackle specific brand problems. They have ideas for apps that would enable people to participate when mobile and ideas for games that would help to drive participation. And they want mechanisms that help to improve creativity, including a greater use of video interaction. While they address the issue of rewards, which they would like to be based on level of participation, it seems clear from the suggested themes that intrinsics are clearly the most important. This comes through strongly in a theme that was suggested and then honed, called 'You the Researcher'. We saw elements of this type of innovation in the Orange co-creation project but the team that developed 'You the Researcher' has taken the concept further.

The insight from the community team that worked on the idea was that people want to get closer to the brands they like, to share their views and to become brand insiders. They also want to feel that they can actively contribute to the development of the brand and to realize their own potential in the process. To achieve this the recommendation is that people should have the opportunity to learn to be ethnographers, observe the world around them and to then bring those observations back to the community. The community would have an area where people could share what they had seen and upload images, recordings and films, something they were used to doing with social media (see Figure 10.2).

FIGURE 10.2   You the researcher

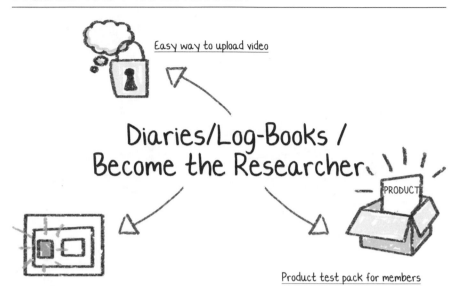

It seems to us that this idea, and the many others developed by the community, crystallize the arguments made in this book. Working together, people have the will and the creativity to be active contributors to the brands they buy and use. If managers are active in creating genuinely interactive experiences and learning from them, they will become better innovators and value creators.

Notes

1   Herzberg, F (2003) 'One More Time: How Do You Motivate Employees.' *Harvard Business Review* **81**(1) p 86

BIBLIOGRAPHY

Agamben, G (1993) *The Coming Community*. (La communita che viene, Enaudi, Turin, 1990) Trans. Hardt, M, University of Minnesota Press, Minneapolis

Amabile, T M and Khaire, M (2008) 'Creativity and the Role of the Leader.' *Harvard Business Review* 86(10)

Anker, M (2009) *The Ethics of Uncertainty: Aporetic Openings* Atropos Press, New York

Baker, A C, Jensen P J, Kolb, D A (2005) 'Conversation as Learning Experience.' *Management Learning* 36(4)

Bakhtin, M (1984) *Rabelais and His World*, Trans. Iswolsky, H, Indiana University Press, Bloomington, Indiana

Balibar, E (2008) *Spinoza and Politics*. (Spinoza et la politique, Presses Universitaires de France, 1985), Trans. Snowdon, P, Verso, London

Blanchot, M (1988) *The Unavowable Community*. (La Communauté Inavouable, Les Editions de Minuit, 1983) Trans. Joris, P, Station Hill, Barrytown, New York

Bødker, S and Grønbæk, K (1990) 'Cooperative Prototyping: Users and Designers in Mutual Activity.' Draft paper submitted for *International Journal of Man-Machine Studies*, special issue on CSCW

Bohm, D (2004) *On Creativity*. Routledge Classics, London

Breton, A (1924) *Manifesto of Surrealism*

Brown, T (2008) 'Design Thinking.' *Harvard Business Review* 86(6)

Burns, T and Stalker, G M (1994) *The Management of Innovation*. Oxford University Press, New York

Carriere, J-C and Eco, U (2011) *This Is Not the End of the Book*. (Ne pensez pas vous débarrasser des livres, 2009. Éditions Grasset & Fasquelle) Trans. McLean, P, Harvill Secker, London

Catmull, E (2008) 'How Pixar Fosters Collective Creativity.' *Harvard Business Review* 86(9)

Chan, K W and Mauborgne, R (2003) 'Tipping Point Leadership', *Harvard Business Review* 81(4)

Chan, K W and Mauborgne, R (2005) *Blue Ocean Strategy: How to Create Uncontested Market Space and Make the Competition Irrelevant*. Harvard Business School Press, Boston, Mass

Chesbrough, H (2006) *Open Innovation: The New Imperative for Creating and Profiting from Technology*. Harvard Business School Press, Boston, Mass

Chiles, T H, Tuggle, C S, McMullen, J S, Bierman, L and Greening, D W (2010) 'Dynamic Creation: Extending the Radical Austrian Approach to Entrepreneurship.' *Organization Studies* 31(1)

Chomsky, N (1998) *On Language*, The New Press, New York

Chomsky, N and Foucault, M (2006) *The Chomsky-Foucault Debate on Human Nature*. The New Press, New York

Collins, J and Porras, J (1998) *Built to Last: Successful Habits of Visionary Companies*. Random House Business Books, London

Cova, B and Dalli, D (2009) 'Working Consumers: The Next Step in Marketing Theory.' *Marketing Theory* 9(3)

Cova, B, Kozinets, R and Shankar, A (2007) *Consumer Tribes*. Butterworth Heinemann, Oxford

Csikszentmihalyi, M (1999) 'A Systems Perspective on Creativity' in *Creative Management and Development* (3rd edition). ed. Henry, J, Sage Publications, London

Debray, R (2000) *Transmitting Culture*. (Transmettre, 1997, Editions Odile Jacob). Trans. Rauth, E, Columbia University Press, New York

Delanda, M (2002) *Intensive Science and Virtual Philosophy*. Continuum, London

Deleuze, G and Guattari, F (2003) *What Is Philosophy?* (Qu'est-ce que la philosophie?, 1991) Trans. Burchell, G and Tomlinson, H, Verso, London

Dodgson, M, Gann, D and Salter, A (2005) *Think, Play, Do: Technology, Innovation and Organization*. Oxford University Press, Oxford

Douglas, M (1966) (2002) *Purity and Danger*. Routledge and Kegan Paul, London, Routledge Classics, London

Doz, Y and Kosonen, M (2008) *Fast Strategy: How Strategic Agility Will Help You Stay Ahead of the Game*. Pearson Education, Harlow, UK

Eco, U (1962) 'The Poetics of the Open Work' in *Participation*, eds Bishop, C, Whitechapel and The MIT Press, London and Cambridge, Mass

Ehrenzweig, A (2000) *The Hidden Order of Art*, Phoenix Press, London

Ekvall, G (1997) 'Organizational Conditions and Levels of Creativity' in *Creative Management and Development* (3rd edition). ed. Henry, J, Sage Publications, London

Freeman, R E, Harrison, J S and Wicks, A C (2007) *Managing for Stakeholders: Survival, Reputation and Success*. Yale University Press, New Haven, CT

Friedrich, R, Peterson, M and Koster, A (2011) 'The Rise of Generation C.' *Strategy+Business* 62

Fukuyama, F (2000) 'Social Capital' in *Culture Matters*. eds Harrison, L and Huntington, S P, Basic Books, New York

Gabor, A (2009) 'The Promise (and Perils) of Open Collaboration.' *Strategy+Business* 56

Gagliardi, P(2006) 'Exploring the Aesthetic Side of Organizational Life' in *The Sage Handbook of Organization Studies*, eds Clegg, S, Hardy, C, Lawrence, T and Nord, W, Sage, Thousand Oaks, California

Grønbæk, K, Kyng, M and Mogensen, P (1997) 'Toward a Cooperative Experimental System Development Approach' in *Computers and Design in Context*. eds Kyng, M and Mathiassen, L, The MIT Press, Cambridge, Mass

Hatch, M J and Schultz, M (2010) 'Toward a Theory of Brand Co-Creation with Implications for Brand Governance.' *Journal of Brand Management* 17(8)

Heidegger, M (1962) *Being and Time*. (Sein und Zeit, Max Niemeyer Verlag, Tübingen, 1927) Trans. Macquarrie, J and Robinson, E, Blackwell, Oxford

Hemetsberger, A and Reinhardt, C (2009) 'Collective Development in Open-Source Communities: An Activity Theoretical Perspective on Successful Online Collaboration.' *Organization Studies* 30(9)

Hemp, P and Stewart, T A (2004) 'Leading Change When Business Is Good: An Interview with Samuel J Palmisano.' *Harvard Business Review*

Herzberg, F (2003) 'One More Time: How Do You Motivate Employees.' *Harvard Business Review* 81(1)

Hume, D (1969) *A Treatise of Human Nature*. First published 1739/1740. Penguin, London

Iglesias, O, Singh, J J and Batista-Foguet, J M (2011) 'The role of brand experience and affective commitment in determining brand loyalty.' *Journal of Brand Management*, 18(8)

Ind, N (2007) *Living the Brand: How to Transform Every Member of Your Organization into a Brand Champion* (3rd edition). Kogan Page, London

Ind, N and Bjerke, R (2007) 'The Concept of Participatory Market Orientation: An Organisation-Wide Approach to Enhancing Brand Equity.' *Journal of Brand Management* **15**

Ind, N and Watt, C (2004) *Inspiration: Capturing the Creative Potential of Your Organisation*. Palgrave, Basingstoke, Hants

Jaruzelski, B and Dehoff, K (2010) 'The Global Innovation 1000: How the Top Innovators Keep Winning.' *Strategy+Business* **61**

Johnson, S (2010) *Where Good Ideas Come From: The Natural History of Innovation*. Allen Lane, London

Kirton, M J (1984) 'Adaptors and Innovators: Why New Initiatives Get Blocked' in *Creative Management and Development* (3rd edition). ed. Henry, J, Sage Publications, London

Kornberger, M (2010) *Brand Society: How Brands Transform Management and Lifestyle*. Cambridge University Press, Cambridge, UK

Kozinets, R V, Hemetsberger, A and Schau, H J (2008) 'The Wisdom of Consumer Crowds: Collective Innovation in the Age of Networked Marketing.' *Journal of Macromarketing* **28**(4)

Lafley, A G and Charan, R (2008) *The Game-Changer: How You Can Drive Revenue and Profit Growth with Innovation*. Crown Business, New York

Leander, K (2009) *Inside Steve's Brain*. Penguin Books, London

Lindblom, C E (1959) 'The Science of Muddling Through', *Public Administration Review* **19**(2) pp 79–88

Luhmann, N (2003) 'Organization' in *Autopoietic Organization Theory: Drawing on Niklas Luhmann's Social Systems Perspective*. eds Bakken, T and Hernes, T, Abstrakt Forlag, Oslo

Magala, S (2009) *The Management of Meaning in Organizations*. Palgrave, Basingstoke, Hants

Matthing, J, Sandén, B and Edvardsson, B (2004) 'New service development learning from and with customers.' *International Journal of Service Industry Management* **15**(5)

Merleau-Ponty, M (2002) *Phenomenology of Perception*. (Phénomenologie de la perception, Gallimard, Paris, 1945), Trans. Smith, C, Routledge Classics, Abingdon, Oxon

Mintzberg, H, Ahlstrand, B and Lampel, J (1998) *Strategy Safari*. FT Prentice Hall, Harlow, Essex

Muniz Jr, A M and O'Guinn, T C (2001) 'Brand Community.' *Journal of Consumer Research*, **27**(4)

Nancy, J-L (2002) *Hegel: The Restlessness of the Negative*. (Hegel: L'inquiétude du négatif, Hachette Littératures, 1997) Trans. Smith, J and Miller, S, University of Minnesota Press, Minneapolis

Nonaka, I and Hirotaka, T (1995) 'Organizational Knowledge Creation' in *Creative Management and Development* (3rd edition). ed. Henry, J, Sage Publications, London

Osborne, T (2003) 'Against 'Creativity': A Philistine Rant.' *Economy & Society* **32**(4)

Payne, A, Storbacka, K, Frow, P and Knox, S (2009) 'Co-Creating Brands: Diagnosing and Designing the Relationship Experience.' *Journal of Business Research* **62**

Petersen, R A 'In search of authenticity.' *Journal of Management Studies* **42**(5)

Porter, R (2000) *Enlightenment: Britain and the Creation of the Modern World.* Allen Lane, The Penguin Press, London

Potts, J, Hartley, J, Banks, J, Burgess, J, Cobcroft, R, Cunningham, S, Montgomery, L (2008) 'Consumer Co-Creation and Situated Creativity.' *Industry and Innovation* **15**(5)

Ramaswamy, V and Gouillart, F, (2010) *The Power of Co-Creation: Build It with Them to Boost Growth, Productivity, and Profits.* Free Press, New York

Raymond, E S. (1999) *The Cathedral and the Bazaar: Musings on Linux and Open Source by an Accidental Revolutionary.* O'Reilly, Sebastopol, California

Ries, A and Ries, L, (1998) *The 22 Immutable Laws of Branding: How to Build a Product or Service into a World-Class Brand.* Harper Business, New York

Ronell, A, (2003) *Stupidity.* University of Illinois Press, Urbana and Chicago

Ronell, A, (2005) *The Test Drive.* University of Illinois Press, Urbana and Chicago

Schau, H, Jensen, M, Albert, M Jr and Arnould, E J (2009) 'How Brand Community Practices Create Value.' *Journal of Marketing* **73**(5)

Schmied, W (2006) *Francis Bacon, Commitment and Conflict.* Trans. Ormrod, J, Prestel Verlag, Munich, Germany

Schouten, J, Martin, D and McAlexander, J (2007) 'The Evolution of a Subculture of Consumption' in *Consumer Tribes,* eds Cova, B, Kozinets, R and Shankar, A Butterworth Heinemann, Oxford

Singer, I (2007) *Ingmar Bergman, Cinematic Philosopher: Reflections on His Creativity.* MIT Press, Cambridge, Mass

Spinoza, B de. *Tractatus Politicus.* Rendered into HTML and Text by Jon Roland of the Constitution Society. Available at: http://www.constitution.org/bs/poltreat.txt. 1998

Statler, M, Roos, J and Victor, B (2002) 'Ain't Misbehavin': Taking Play Seriously in Organizations.' *Imagination Lab Foundation,* **28**

Svendsen, L (2005) *A Philosophy of Boredom.* (Kjedsomhetens filosofi, Universitetsforlaget, Oslo, 1999) Trans. Irons, J, Reaktion Books, London

Thyssen, O (2003) 'Luhmann and Management: A Critique of the Management Theory in Organisation Und Entscheidung' in *Autopoietic Organization Theory: Drawing on Niklas Luhmann's Social Systems Perspective,* eds Bakken, T and Hernes, T, Abstrakt Forlag, Oslo

Tuqan, Y T (2010) 'If Brands (and Governments) Don't Do Their Job, Someone Else Will Do It for Them.' *Journal of the Medinge Group,* **4**

Vargo, S L and Lusch, R F (2004) 'Evolving to a New Dominant Logic for Marketing.' *Journal of Marketing* **68**

von Hippel, E (2006) *Democratizing Innovation.* The MIT Press, Cambridge, Mass

Watt, C and Ind, N (2011) 'Big Chef-Little Chef: The Bear-Traps and Pitfalls That Can Hinder Design Thinking.' *Design Principles and Practices* **5**(2)

Weick, K E (2003) 'Organizational Design and the Gehry Experience.' *Journal of Management Enquiry* **12**(1)

Weick, K E (2006) 'The Role of Imagination in the Organizing of Knowledge.' *European Journal of Information Systems* **15**

Zupancic, A (2008) *The Odd One In: On Comedy.* The MIT Press, Cambridge, Mass

INDEX